PRAGMATISM:
A GUIDE FOR THE PERPLEXED

Robert B. Talisse and Scott F. Aikin

D1603282

continuum

Continuum International Publishing Group
The Tower Building   80 Maiden Lane
11 York Road   Suite 704
London SE1 7NX   New York NY 10038

www.continuumbooks.com

© Robert B. Talisse and Scott F. Aikin 2008

British Library Cataloguing-in-Publication Data
A catalogue record for this book is available from the Library of Congress.

ISBN: HB: 0-8264-9857-4
       978-0-8264-9857-1

       PB: 0-8264-9858-2
       978-0-8264-9858-8

Library of Congress Cataloging-in-Publication Data
A catalog record is available from the Library of Congress.

Typeset by Newgen Imaging Systems Pvt Ltd, Chennai, India
Printed and bound in Great Britain by MPG Books Ltd, Cornwall

CONTENTS

ACKNOWLEDGMENTS

This book is the product of years of earnest struggle to figure out what is living and what is dead in pragmatism. Our thinking on the topics addressed in this book proceeded mostly by way of long conversations and arguments which benefited from the participation of many of our friends and colleagues. We would especially like to thank Jody Azzouni, James Bednar, Antonio Bendezu, Caleb Clanton, Allen Coates, Matt Cotter, Josh Crites, Cornelis de Waal, Michael Eldridge, Richard Gale, Lenn Goodman, Peter Hare, Micah Hester, David Hildebrand, Charlie Hobbs, Brendan Hogan, Michael Hodges, Angelo Juffras, Chris King, John Lachs, Joe Margolis, Mason Marshall, Cheryl Misak, Jonathan Neufeld, John Peterman, Brian Ribeiro, Robert Tempio, and Jeffrey Tlumak. We thank Tyler Zimmer for his help in producing the index. In the course of our work, we also incurred personal debts which we should like to acknowledge. Robert Talisse thanks Joanne Billett. Scott Aikin thanks his wife, Susan Foxman, and his daughters, Madeleine and Iris.

CHAPTER 1

THE ORIGINS OF PRAGMATISM

PRELIMINARIES

What Is This Book About?

The terms *pragmatism, pragmatic,* and *pragmatist* are commonly used to denote a commitment to success in practical affairs, to 'getting things done'. Pragmatists are driven not by principle, but by the desire to achieve their ends. Hence pragmatists have little interest in abstraction, idealization, nitpicking argument, or *theory* of any sort; they have no time for these because they are fixed on practical tasks. A *pragmatist* is hence a bargainer, a negotiator, a *doer*, rather than a seeker of truth, a wonderer, or a *thinker*. We might say, then, that *pragmatism* is the opposite of philosophy.

This is a philosophy book, and the pragmatism with which we are concerned is not the pragmatism of common parlance. Pragmatism in the sense which concerns us is the name for something distinctively philosophical. But what? Is pragmatism a *school* of philosophy organized around a single doctrine in the way that we might say that, for example, *Stoicism* is a school? Not quite. Although there are doctrinal similarities and channels of influence among all pragmatist philosophers, the differences among them make it difficult to see them as constituting a school. Is pragmatism a philosophical *theory*? Not exactly. It is difficult to point to a single philosophical claim to which all pragmatists subscribe. Is it a historical trend or movement within the history of philosophy? Although pragmatism arose out of specific conditions in the United States at the close of the nineteenth century and is a distinctively *American* philosophy, it is not bound to any particular cultural or historical milieu. So what is this book about?

Even the most preliminary attempt to say what pragmatism is raises considerable difficulties. Even if we confine ourselves to those contemporary philosophers who use the term to describe their views, we find a cacophony of distinct and often opposed doctrines, ranging from the hard-nosed naturalism of W. V. O. Quine to the playful and frustrating postmodernism of Richard Rorty, the economic reductionism of Richard Posner, and the prophetic social activism of Cornel West.

As this brief list suggests, philosophers who embrace the term pragmatism disagree over central and substantive philosophical matters. They also disagree about *what pragmatism is*. Some say that pragmatism is a thesis about meaning, reference, communication, or language itself. Others claim that pragmatism is an epistemological proposal, an account of knowledge, belief, justification, inquiry, or truth. Some hold it is a metaphysical perspective, a view about reality, nature, what there is, what we should say there is, or what we should say about what natural science says there is. Still others deny that pragmatism is a philosophical account of anything in particular. Among these philosophers, some say pragmatism is a *method* of doing philosophy. Others claim it is a *stance* one might take toward traditional philosophical problems. According to some, pragmatism is an *attitude* one takes toward philosophy itself. Some have held that pragmatism is a kind of intellectual *therapy*, an antidote to the human compulsion to obsess over the traditional questions of philosophy.

In light of all of this, it seems that maybe the only thing to do is to agree with Richard Rorty, who observed that pragmatism is 'a vague, ambiguous, and overworked word' (1982: 160). But accepting Rorty's obviously correct assessment of the situation gets us no closer to an answer to our original question: What is this book about?

Pragmatism as a Living Philosophy

It is especially fitting that this book bears the subtitle *A Guide for the Perplexed*. Perplexity concerning the nature of pragmatism will persist throughout this book, and we shall not attempt to dispel it; that is, we shall not in these pages attempt to sort out the question of what pragmatism is. Where necessary, we shall refer to it as a *philosophy*, in full acknowledgment of the ambiguity of that term.

One might be tempted to see our inability to precisely circumscribe our topic as a kind of philosophical failure on the part of the pragmatists themselves. One might think that the fact that we cannot set out from a clear definition of pragmatism indicates that pragmatist philosophy is *itself* unclear and imprecise. To be sure, pragmatists are not immune to unclear and imprecise thinking. But no philosopher enjoys such immunity. The lack of a precise definition of pragmatism does not derive from some excess of imprecision on the part of pragmatist philosophers; rather, it is a product of the fact that, relatively speaking, pragmatism is a *new* phenomenon on the philosophical scene. It has been just over 100 years since the term was first used in print in a philosophical context. In the history of philosophy, a century is hardly enough time for a philosophy to calcify into a unified intellectual program. Accordingly, we would be hard pressed to state with precision the meaning of any of the terms used to designate the philosophies that arose in the twentieth century: terms such as *existentialism* and *phenomenology* and *analytic philosophy* admit of similar ambiguity. We can point to figures, texts, and arguments that more or less *characterize* each of these, but we cannot say more than this. Perhaps in another century's time we will be able to more precisely delimit the meaning of *pragmatism*, in the way in which we now can talk about *absolute idealism*, *British empiricism*, and *Cartesian rationalism* as distinctive philosophical programs. But for now, the ambiguity cannot be eliminated.

This state of affairs is not lamentable. The resistance of pragmatism to precise definition is a mark of its vitality, an indication that it is a *living philosophy* rather than a historical relic. This means that questions concerning its principal contentions, major themes, and central arguments are still *open questions*, questions that pragmatists are still working through. Pragmatism, whatever it is, is still working itself out, still trying to figure out what it is.

Our aim in this book is to survey a wide range of philosophical positions that have been characterized as pragmatist. We present these various versions of pragmatism as responses to leading questions of philosophy. Accordingly, we will survey the leading pragmatist options in metaphysics, epistemology, ethics, and political philosophy, while giving special attention to the topics of truth and environmental ethics. Our objective throughout is to present each pragmatist position in its best light; however, we are also concerned to show how each must confront hard cases and powerful objections from its philosophical competitors. In these pages pragmatism will emerge as a collection of more or less loosely connected philosophical themes, arguments, and commitments; we will show that while each version of pragmatism has its distinctive insights and virtues, none can claim to be the last word on the philosophical problems to which it is addressed.

Hence we shall find that not only is the nature of pragmatism an open question, but there is also an open question about whether any version of pragmatism is philosophically viable. This is not to say that pragmatism is a philosophical dead end. That pragmatism has not been vindicated does not mean that it has been vanquished. Instead, it means that, like all living philosophies, the ultimate fate of pragmatism is yet to be determined. To use the language of the pragmatist William James, we will see that pragmatism is a *live option* in philosophy, but certainly not the only option. Such is the mark of a living philosophy: its ultimate fortune is yet an open question, something that could be determined only within the processes of ongoing philosophical argument.

Our Approach

Our discussion will proceed by way of an examination of the philosophical problems to which pragmatists have applied themselves. In each case we try to present the most powerful version of the arguments offered by various pragmatists in favor of their positions. But we also give considerable attention to the objections and challenges posed by the opponents of pragmatism; in fact, we typically conclude our discussions by giving the critic the last word. To be sure, we do this not in order to suggest that pragmatism has been defeated. Rather we aim to indicate to our reader where there is still work for the pragmatist to do. In some places, we will be quite sharp. This is for two reasons. First, we think pragmatist views can be improved, and feeling the pinch of a philosophical difficulty with one's arguments is the best spur to do the requisite work. We ourselves work on the problems we pose here, and we do so precisely because we see pragmatism as engaged with difficult philosophical issues. The second reason why we pose the criticisms so starkly is that we think pragmatists can be better, too. There is a regrettable narrative dominant in the pragmatist tradition which holds that although there once were philosophical problems of the sort traditional philosophers struggled with, such problems no longer exist because pragmatism has dissolved them. According to this narrative, those not working in the pragmatist idiom have simply missed the boat. But nonpragmatist philosophers often have answers to and criticisms of pragmatist views. Further, many pragmatist insights have been integrated into mainstream philosophical programs well beyond those considered pragmatist. In short, pragmatists are members of an intellectual community, not just of fellow pragmatists, but of philosophers whose concerns, objections, and questions merit response. The heat with which we pose our challenges is proportioned to how urgent we take the need for a response to be.

It should be acknowledged from the outset that our approach in this book runs counter to the way of presenting pragmatism that has become standard. Most commentators on the history of pragmatism present some version of the following story: Pragmatism was initiated in the late 1800s by Charles Sanders Peirce, flourished in the United States throughout the first half of the twentieth century through the work of William James and John Dewey, fell into disfavor or obscurity following World War II due to the influence of a rival philosophical orientation often called *analytic philosophy*, and was revived in the 1980s mainly by Richard Rorty.

We think that this story is in many respects misleading. In the first place, it overlooks the fact that many of the developments that it associates with the analytic style of philosophizing that rose to prominence in the years following World War II are self-professedly descendants of the ideas and arguments found in the work of the founding pragmatists, namely, Peirce, James, and Dewey. As we will see in the coming chapters, pragmatist insights and arguments are alive and well in the 'analytic' philosophies that the standard story casts as pragmatism's philosophical nemesis.

Second, the standard story invites the idea that the so-called revival of pragmatism is primarily a *retrieval* of the canonical expressions of pragmatism in the work of Peirce, James, and Dewey. Accordingly, a sizeable portion of the recent work on pragmatism is devoted to policing the philosophical purposes to which the ideas of the founding pragmatists are put. Hence Richard Rorty, the philosopher uniformly acknowledged among those who promote this story to be the main force behind the revival of pragmatism, is more frequently chastised for his alleged misreading of Dewey than engaged with at the level of his philosophical commitments. One gets the sense that those invested in the claim that pragmatism has been revived are more interested in *preserving* the philosophical ideas of the founders than in making fresh philosophical advances or having new philosophical thoughts. But any revival of pragmatism (assuming for the moment that there was one) worth attending to surely must amount to more than a revival of interest in the *historical* figures most commonly associated with pragmatism. Recall that the narrative claims that Rorty instigated a *philosophical* revival of pragmatism, a renewed interest in the claims and arguments associated with pragmatism, not merely an invitation to scholastic veneration of the founding pragmatists.

Third, and most importantly, the standard story tends to underplay – or in extreme cases, flatly deny – the degree to which the original pragmatists were philosophically divided over core issues. That is, the story tends to present pragmatism as a unified philosophical school, organized around the succession of headmasters, each of whom simply carried further the thought of his predecessor. Thus, H. S. Thayer writes,

> In a word, pragmatism is a method of philosophizing often identified as a theory of meaning first stated by Charles Peirce in the 1870's; revived primarily as a theory of truth in 1898 by William James; and further developed, expanded, and disseminated by John Dewey. (1981: 5)

On Thayer's view, pragmatism is essentially the philosophical project of working out Peirce's theory of meaning. Accordingly, the story of pragmatism, as told by Thayer, is the story of developing and disseminating Peirce's views.

But the true story is not this simple. As we'll see in the next section, the founding pragmatists disagreed sharply about the scope and application of Peirce's theory of meaning; these disagreements gave rise to striking philosophical differences among them. Indeed, the differences were so stark that Peirce was led in 1905 to renounce the term pragmatism and rechristen his philosophy *pragmaticism*, a word he hoped would be 'ugly enough to be safe from kidnappers' (CP, 5.415).[1] Our account of the history of pragmatism must not rely too heavily upon there being a *doctrinal* unity among the founding pragmatists. But this is precisely what the standard narrative encourages.

John Smith has offered a more nuanced reading of the career of pragmatism, one that recognizes the doctrinal differences to which we have alluded. Smith writes,

> The individual differences marking the thought of the classical pragmatist philosophers are undeniable: Peirce's orientation is logical and metaphysical, James follows the path of psychology and personal experience, [and] Dewey stresses the biological and functional structures in individual life and society. (1999: 3)

Smith then picks up the theme of doctrinal unity, writing that '[t]hese differences, however, must not be allowed to obscure the powerful presence of a basic outlook that all shared and identified as pragmatism' (1999: 3). He characterizes this 'basic outlook' as follows

> This outlook stands for some doctrines about the nature of things, but it also includes a way of thinking, a spirit of adventure, and above all, the belief that ideas make a difference in the world and are not merely to be contemplated but must be set to work guiding what we think and do. (1999: 3)

To be sure, Smith's view is certainly closer to the mark than Thayer's. However, if Smith is correct to say that the shared basic outlook of all pragmatists is constituted 'above all' by the view that ideas make a difference in the world and 'must be set to work in guiding what we think and do', then pragmatism is in no way novel or original or even *distinguishable* from other philosophical movements. To see this, consider that figures in the history of philosophy otherwise as opposed as Aristotle, Rousseau, Bentham, and Marx all share this basic outlook with the pragmatists. Moreover, other movements in twentieth-century philosophy that are often viewed as decidedly antipragmatist – such as logical positivism and critical theory – also describe themselves as committed to the view that 'ideas must be set to work guiding what we think and do'. So whereas Thayer's view suffers the vice of understating disagreement, Smith's tends to surrender the claim that the classical pragmatists were offering a *distinctive* philosophical approach.

Despite these defects, most treatments of the history pragmatism proceed along Thayer–Smith lines. Accordingly, many books introducing pragmatism begin with Peirce, and follow out, in historical order, the progression to James, Dewey, and eventually Rorty and his contemporaries. We have already indicated the ways in which our approach rejects this model. Nonetheless, even though our discussion throughout will be problems based rather than historical, *something* must be said about the first pragmatists in order to put the following chapters in context.

CONTESTATION OVER PRAGMATISM

How Many Pragmatisms?

Roughly a century ago, A. O. Lovejoy set out to 'discriminate all the more important doctrines going under the name of pragmatism' (1908: 13). Taking William James's 1898 essay on 'Philosophical Conceptions and Practical Results' as marking the inauguration of pragmatism as a completed doctrine, Lovejoy reasoned that pragmatism's second decade should begin with an earnest effort to 'attach some single and stable meaning' to the term (1908: 1). Through a careful analysis of key articulations of pragmatism, Lovejoy identified 13 logically distinct and independent theses, each claiming to constitute the core of the pragmatist doctrine. Since these 13 did not make a consistent set, Lovejoy proposed that each ostensibly pragmatist thesis 'should manifestly be given a name of its own', for this would be the only way to avoid 'confusion in future discussion' (1908: 28). Lovejoy confessed that he had neither 'the necessary ingenuity' nor 'the ambition' to propose 'a nomenclature so extensive' (1908: 29).

It is reasonable to suspect that the number of pragmatisms in currency today far exceeds 13. To our knowledge, no one has yet taken up Lovejoy's project of distinguishing and naming each distinct variety, and we will not attempt to do so here. But we do want to pick up on our claim from the previous section that pragmatism has always been a site of contestation, and that the founding pragmatists were often at odds with each other concerning central philosophical questions. In the following, we take a brief tour through the distinct pragmatisms of Peirce, James, and Dewey. By examining the main contours of their respective pragmatisms, we will be able to see clearly the ways in which they differ.

How James Kidnapped Peirce

It is natural to follow Lovejoy in taking William James's 'Philosophical Conceptions and Practical Results', to mark the inauguration of pragmatism as a philosophy. In that essay, James explicitly takes himself to be launching a new movement; he claims to be an intellectual trailblazer offering 'the most likely direction in which *to start* upon the trail of truth', indicating that in his judgment the true task of philosophy had not yet been attempted (WWJ, 347; our emphasis).[2] Oddly, by the time we hit the essay's fifth paragraph, we are referred by James back 20 years to an 1878 article by Charles Sanders Peirce titled 'How to Make Our Ideas Clear'. James claims that, in that essay, Peirce first expressed 'the principle of pragmatism' (WWJ, 348). However, in his own treatment of Peirce's principle, James confesses that pragmatism 'should be expressed more broadly than Mr. Peirce expresses it' (WWJ, 348). Apparently, this broadening did not suit Peirce. In 1905, he wrote of James's 'Philosophical Conceptions' paper that it 'pushed' the pragmatic maxim 'to such extremes as to give us pause' (CP, 5.4). As we mentioned earlier, in another 1905 paper, Peirce expressed his dissatisfaction with 'what other pragmatists have written'; he rebaptized his philosophy *pragmaticism*, a term he thought so 'ugly' that no one would want to kidnap it (CP, 5.415). In this section, we present an account of what Peirce found unsatisfactory in James's expression of pragmatism.

In 'How to Make Our Ideas Clear', Peirce formulates the view of meaning that is the core of his pragmatism and that provides the touchstone for many subsequent varieties of pragmatism. Peirce writes,

> To develop [a thought's] meaning, we have simply to determine what habits it produces, for what a thing means is simply what habits it involves. (CP, 5.400)

By 'habit' Peirce means a standard course of action undertaken in response to specific conditions. For any thought, then, one may extract its complete meaning by drawing out the proposals for action that it suggests. This thesis has come to be known as the *pragmatic maxim*. Peirce expresses the idea thus:

> Consider what effects, that might conceivably have practical bearings, we conceive the object of our conception to have. Then our

conception of these effects is the whole of our conception of the object. (CP, 5.402)

According to Peirce's maxim, we discern the meaning of a proposition[3] by formulating a conditional of the following form,

If one were to perform action A, one would observe result B.

To use Peirce's own example, if one says of some object, X, that it is *hard*, one means that it would not be scratched by many other objects (CP, 5.403); that is, 'X is *hard*' means 'If one were to rub X against many other objects, X would not be scratched'. Similarly, the proposition, 'X is *heavy*' means that 'If X were left without support, X would fall' (CP, 5.403).[4]

Peirce hence connects meaning to 'what is tangible and conceivably practical' (CP, 5.400); on his view, the meaning of a proposition is essentially a proposal, or a prediction, regarding the functioning of its object within our experience. Indeed, Peirce held that such proposals were *exhaustive* of a proposition's meaning:

If one can identify accurately all the conceivable phenomena which the affirmation or denial of a concept could imply, one will have therein a complete definition of the concept, *and there is absolutely nothing more in it*. (CP, 5.412)

Importantly, insofar as the pragmatic maxim provides an *exhaustive* analysis of a proposition's meaning, it also provides a criterion for meaninglessness. The maxim entails that any proposition that cannot be cashed out in terms of the observable effects of acting with its object is *ipso facto* meaningless. Accordingly, Peirce thought that many of the traditional positions in philosophy, especially metaphysics, were literally meaningless. For example, he argues that the Thomistic doctrine of transubstantiation, which holds that during Mass a priest actually changes the substance of bread and wine into flesh and blood without changing any of their attributes, is 'senseless jargon' (CP, 5. 401). In fact, Peirce saw pragmatism as 'merely method of ascertaining the meanings of hard words and abstract concepts' (CP, 5.464). He held that this a method 'will serve to show that almost every proposition of ontological metaphysics is either meaningless gibberish . . . or else downright absurd' (CP, 5.423). That is, according to Peirce, pragmatism was essentially an antimetaphysical strategy, a way of dismissing the 'make-believes' (CP, 5.416) of previous philosophizing and of keeping open the road of proper inquiry.[5] Peirce thought that once the road of inquiry is swept clear of 'meaningless gibberish', all that would remain is 'a series of problems capable of investigation by the observational methods of the true sciences' (CP, 5.423).

To be sure, pragmatism was not the whole of Peirce's philosophy. Peirce's philosophical work spans nearly every major topic and issue within the discipline, from logic and (scientific) metaphysics to theology, cosmology, semiotics, and aesthetics. Yet pragmatism was the *beginning* or the *core* of Peirce's philosophy; it was the method by which he thought philosophy could break from its error-ridden past.

James saw things differently. In 'Philosophical Conceptions and Practical Results', James employs Peirce's pragmatic maxim, which he expresses as follows:

If there were any part of a thought that made no difference in the thought's practical consequences, then that part would be no proper element of the thought's significance. (WWJ, 349)

James continues,

The effective meaning of any philosophical proposition can always be brought down to some particular consequence in our future practical experience. (WWJ, 349)

In these statements, James broadens Peirce's maxim in a way that is subtle but consequential. Like Peirce, James appeals to a proposition's 'practical consequences' to determine its meaning. We begin to see the divergence between James and Peirce, however, by examining the way in which James construes the notion of a practical consequence. Whereas Peirce limits the notion of a practical consequence to that which is 'tangible and conceivably practical' (CP, 5.400), James designs his pragmatism to include within a given proposition's pragmatic meaning the psychological effects of *believing* it. In short, James broadened Peirce's maxim by *psychologizing* it.

The psychological character of James's pragmatism is evident in his discussion of the debate between materialists and spiritualists. Noting that debate does *not* concern a difference in sensation or observation (a feature that would render the debate meaningless on Peirce's view), James claims that the dispute is one that concerns psychological *temperament* only. Thus, on James's view, materialism pragmatically means:

> In the vast driftings of the cosmic weather, tho many a jeweled shore appears, and many an enchanted cloud-bank floats away, long lingering ere it be dissolved – even as our world now lingers, for our joy – yet when these transient products are gone, nothing absolutely nothing remains, to represent those particular qualities, those elements of preciousness which that may have enshrined. (WWJ, 354)

Summarizing the materialist position less poetically, James claims that materialism pragmatically means that 'the lower and not the higher forces are the eternal forces' (WWJ, 354).

Contrast this characterization with James's analysis of the pragmatic meaning of the spiritualist position:

> A world with a God in it to say the last word, may indeed burn up or freeze, but we then think of Him as still mindful of the old ideals and sure to bring them elsewhere to fruition; so that, where He is, tragedy is only provisional and partial, and shipwreck and dissolution not the final things. (WWJ, 354)

James concedes that the spiritualist position is 'inferior' in 'clearness' to the materialist position; however, he contends that spiritualism nonetheless has a 'practical superiority' over materialism in that it 'guarantees that an ideal order . . . shall be preserved' (WWJ, 354).

James encapsulates the debate between materialists and spiritualists as follows:

> Here, then, in these different emotional and practical appeals, in there adjustments of our concrete attitudes of hope and expectation, and all the delicate consequences which their differences entail, lie the real meanings of materialism and spiritualism – not in hair-splitting abstractions about matter's inner essence, or about the metaphysical attributes of God. Materialism means simply the denial that the moral order is eternal, and the cutting off of

ultimate hopes; [spiritualism] means the affirmation of an eternal moral order and the letting loose of hope. (WWJ, 354)

James contends that since the 'need for an eternal moral order is one of the deepest needs in our breast' (WWJ, 354), the metaphysical dispute between materialists and spiritualists is easily settled in favor of the latter position. From the perspective of the Jamesian pragmatist, then, the 'true objection' to materialism is that it does not provide a 'permanent warrant for our more ideal interests'; it is not a 'fulfiller of our remotest hopes'; it results in 'utter final wreck and tragedy' (WWJ, 354).

Although the contrast between Peirce's and James's understandings of the pragmatic maxim should be clear, let us consider briefly an example of an issue treated by both Peirce and James in which they propose opposing pragmatic analyses.

In *Pragmatism: A New Name for Some Old Ways of Thinking* (WWJ, 362–472), James takes up the question of transubstantiation. We have already noted that Peirce held that the doctrine was to be discarded as 'meaningless gibberish' (CP, 5.423). However, James contends that the issue of transubstantiation involves 'the only pragmatic application of the substance-idea' (WWJ, 392), the only instance in which the concept of substance has any pragmatic meaning. According to James, if we dismiss the doctrine of transubstantiation, we reject the psychologically potent idea that in the Mass we 'feed upon the very substance of divinity' (WWJ, 392). According to James, the doctrine of transubstantiation is hardly 'meaningless gibberish'; it is a doctrine of 'tremendous effect' (WWJ, 392).

We may capture the difference between Peirce's and James's understandings of the pragmatic maxim in the following way. Peirce held that in order to grasp the meaning of a proposition, one must understand what experiences to expect *were that proposition true*. By contrast, James held that part of the meaning of a proposition (and the full meaning of certain propositions) is constituted by the psychological effects of *believing* it to be true. As we have seen, James, unlike Peirce, is willing to treat as meaningful certain metaphysical propositions that, even if true, would entail no definite implications for observation; in such cases, James contends that the meaning of the proposition consists completely in the psychological implications of *adopting* or *believing* it. Thus, on James's analysis, the ostensibly metaphysical claims about the ultimate nature of reality represented in the competing positions of materialism and spiritualism *say nothing* about the ultimate nature of reality; they instead represent two competing psychological comportments toward the world, namely, hopelessness and hope, respectively.

To put the contrast in more general terms, Peirce saw pragmatism as a way of ridding philosophy of traditional metaphysics by showing that most metaphysical propositions are meaningless. Peirce thought that once the pragmatic maxim had cleared the decks of nonsense and philosophical red herrings, philosophy could be set upon a new and more scientific track. James, however, took pragmatism to be 'primarily a method of *settling* metaphysical disputes that might otherwise be interminable' (WWJ, 377; our emphasis), by first casting the opposing positions as making different psychological appeals, and then selecting the appeal that satisfies best one's psychological needs. Thus, whereas for Peirce pragmatism was simply a logical rule for doing philosophy, for James, pragmatism was *itself* a philosophy.

This conclusion regarding James will strike some as dubious. James claims in *Pragmatism* that pragmatism is 'a method only' that 'does not stand for any special results' (WWJ, 379); he explicitly claims that his pragmatism 'has no dogmas, and no doctrines' (WWJ, 380). He then likens his pragmatism to a 'corridor in a hotel' that houses a broad diversity of intellectual projects and processes. Of this intellectual corridor, James writes,

> Innumerable chambers open out of it. In one you may find a man writing an atheistic volume; in the next some one on his knees praying for faith and strength; in a third a chemist investigating a body's properties. In a fourth a system of idealistic metaphysics is being excogitated; in a fifth, the impossibility of metaphysics is being shown. But they all own the corridor, and all must pass through it if they want a practicable way of getting into or out of their respective rooms. (WWJ, 380)

But James's image of pragmatism as a philosophically neutral space in which all intellectual projects have a home and within which all come into contact with the rest cannot be correct. In the very same lecture, James himself admits that pragmatism is also a theory of truth (WWJ, 381). The details of James's controversial theory of truth cannot be engaged in this chapter, but note that James's view of truth is *opposed* to traditional correspondence and coherence views; consequently, Jamesian pragmatism *does* stand for the result that those alternate theories are in error. More importantly, the bulk of *Pragmatism* is devoted to showing the pragmatic superiority of certain philosophical positions over others. For example, as we have seen above, James thinks that pragmatism is committed to spiritualism over materialism. He devotes the entire third chapter of *Pragmatism* to showing how certain 'metaphysical problems' look when 'pragmatically considered'. As it turns out, James's pragmatism entails a particular view of material substance (WWJ, 392), of personal identity (WWJ, 393), of free will (WWJ, 403), of reality (WWJ, 451), and of religion (WWJ, 466). It is opposed to the 'materialistic bias as ordinary empiricism labors under' (WWJ, 381), to rationalism (WWJ, 439), to determinism (WWJ, 402), and to monism (WWJ, 411).

Despite his claims to the contrary and his metaphor of the corridor, James's pragmatism *does* stand for certain 'special results' (WWJ, 379). How could it be otherwise? If pragmatism is to serve as a method for 'resolving metaphysical disputes that might otherwise be interminable' (WWJ, 377), it simply *must* entail certain doctrines; for if it did not, pragmatism would not resolve any disputes.

Hence we may say that James 'broadened' Peirce's conception in two distinct but related ways. First, James broadened the application of Peirce's maxim by including among the 'practical consequences' of a proposition the *psychological* effects of *believing* it. Second, James broadened what we might call the *domain* of pragmatism, the range of philosophical topics with regard to which pragmatism itself directly entails a position. To be a Jamesian pragmatist is to endorse a wide range of philosophical claims; it is to accept a collection of specific resolutions to standard metaphysical problems. By contrast, Peirce rejects the idea that pragmatism *itself* entails any positive philosophical commitments beyond the pragmatic maxim and its corresponding criterion of meaninglessness. Since, for Peirce, the pragmatic maxim calls us simply to specify the observable effects that would follow were a proposition true, pragmatism does not settle any disputes; rather, it clarifies *what is at issue* in any given dispute, thereby helping us to identify what experiment or action to undertake in order to resolve it. As Peirce himself wrote in a letter to James, 'Pragmatism solves no real problem. It only shows that the supposed problems are not real problems' (CP, 8.25).

Dewey's Response to James

Before moving on to discuss in some detail the respects in which Peirce and Dewey differed over the nature of pragmatism, it is worth dwelling for a moment on the fact that, like Peirce, Dewey also expressed dissatisfaction with James's pragmatism.

At key junctures in his *Pragmatism*, James makes enthusiastic reference to Dewey's work (WWJ, 382; 388; 442). James also laments the fact that Dewey's critics misinterpret him. James reports that Dewey holds the view that 'truth is what gives satisfaction'; James then complains that Dewey is treated by uncharitable critics 'as one who believes in calling everything true which, if it were true, would be pleasant' (WWJ, 442). However, in a 1908 review essay of James's *Pragmatism* titled 'What Pragmatism Means by "Practical"', Dewey criticizes James for misappropriating his work. Dewey writes,

> Since Mr. James has referred to me as saying 'truth is what gives satisfaction', I may remark (apart from the fact that I do not think I ever said that truth is what *gives* satisfaction) that I have never identified any satisfaction with the truth of an idea, save *that* satisfaction which arises when the idea as working hypothesis or tentative method is applied to prior existences in such a way as to fulfill what it intends. (MW4: 109; italics in the original)[6]

Furthermore, Dewey implicitly rejects James's characterization of pragmatism as 'primarily a method of settling metaphysical disputes that might otherwise be interminable' (WWJ, 377). According to Dewey, James's entire strategy presumes the *prima facie* validity of standing metaphysical disputes. Against this, Dewey claims,

> For myself, I have no hesitation in saying that it seems unpragmatic for pragmatism to content itself with finding out the value of a conception whose own inherent significance pragmatism has not first determined. (MW4: 107)

According to Dewey, pragmatism is primarily a critical tool for assessing the value of certain traditional philosophical problems. Dewey judged many of the standard philosophical disputes to be pseudoproblematic; he argued that the very terms and categories they presupposed were objectionable and ought to be dismissed. According to Dewey, we 'do not solve' the standard philosophical problems, 'we get over them' (MW4: 14); that is, Dewey held that pragmatists should not attempt to 'settle metaphysical disputes that might otherwise be interminable', they should *dispose* of them. In this way, Dewey follows Peirce in seeing pragmatism not as an *answer* to traditional philosophical problems, but as a method for inoculating ourselves against certain recurring blind alleys in philosophy. However, Dewey, like James, saw pragmatism in more expansive terms than Peirce did; for Dewey, as for James, pragmatism was not merely a method of discerning the meaning of words and propositions, but an entire philosophical system.

Peirce and Dewey: Two Concepts of Inquiry

At first blush, the pragmatisms of Dewey and Peirce seem closely allied. This in large part is due to the fact that both Peirce and Dewey, unlike James, place the concept of *inquiry* (what both would call 'logic') at the center of their pragmatism. Dewey himself was keen to establish the lineage. Like James, Dewey claims to be deeply indebted to Peirce; he describes Peirce as 'the man who more than any other single person is the begetter in philosophy of an attitude and outlook distinctively American' (LW15: 273), and elsewhere credits Peirce with having devised 'the best definition of *truth* from the logical standpoint which is known to me' (LW12: 343; italic in the original). However, although Peirce published a favorable review of one of Dewey's early books on logical theory (CP, 8.188f.), in personal correspondence to Dewey he rejected Dewey's view, claiming that it was 'too loose' and comprised of 'slipshod arguments'.

The companion essay to Peirce's 1878 'How to Make Our Ideas Clear' is his 1877 article, 'The Fixation of Belief'.[7] There, Peirce introduces the doubt-belief model of inquiry that is picked up by Dewey.[8] In this section, we want to draw attention to some crucial contrasts between the theories of inquiry offered by Peirce and Dewey. These contrasts will support the conclusion that, like James before him, Dewey promoted a version of pragmatism that is broader than Peircean pragmatism.

Inquiry, according to Peirce, is the 'struggle' to attain a state of 'belief' from a prior state of 'doubt' (CP, 5.374). 'Belief', on the Peircean model, is a state which 'guides[s] our desires and shape[s] our actions' (CP, 5.371); it is 'a calm and satisfactory state which we do not wish to avoid' (CP, 5.372) which provides a 'more or less sure indication of there being established in our nature some habit which will determine our actions' (CP, 5.371). 'Doubt', on the other hand, 'never has such an effect' as to guide our actions; rather, it marks a disturbance in action. Doubt is the state that results when one is confronted with recalcitrant experience, unexpected or unfamiliar conditions to which current habits of action – that is, current beliefs – are unfit to respond. It is a state in which one feels the need to act in some way, yet finds the conditions under which action must be undertaken sufficiently unfamiliar as to render habitual courses of response inappropriate. Doubt is a state in which one knows not how to act. Consequently, doubt is an 'uneasy state from which we struggle to free ourselves' (CP, 5.372).

Inquiry, then, occurs only when one is confronted with doubt; hence, 'the sole object of inquiry is the settlement of opinion' (CP, 5.375). That is, inquiry is undertaken for the exclusive purpose of eliminating doubt and attaining belief, 'when doubt ceases, mental action on the subject comes to an end' (CP, 5.376).

From this, Peirce reasoned, any process by which doubt is exchanged for belief will qualify as inquiry. In 'The Fixation of Belief', Peirce evaluates various competing methods of inquiry according to a fairly intuitive criterion: We should adopt only that method of inquiry which tends to produce beliefs which are stable. A belief is stable insofar as it does not occasion doubt. Accordingly, the logic of Peirce's argument is clear; he reasons that if the sole objective of inquiry is the destruction of doubt and the production of belief, then that method of inquiry is best which tends to result in beliefs that are unlikely to occasion doubt.

There are several options open to us when we are confronted with doubt. One might, for example, employ the method of *tenacity* (CP, 5.378), and attempt to preserve one's belief by simply ignoring the source of doubt. Alternatively, one could appeal to some *authority* to settle the matter (CP, 5.380), or one could elect to surround oneself with the company of like-minded friends who simply reinforce that which one is inclined to believe (CP, 5.382). According to Peirce, these options all will fail to satisfy, since none will generate beliefs that will not occasion doubt.

Peirce argues that the method of *science* (CP, 5.384), by contrast, is the only inquiry procedure that satisfies his evaluative criterion.[9] Unlike the other methods, all of which attempt to preserve belief by avoiding experiences that might occasion doubt, the scientific method seeks to produce beliefs that can *withstand* the test of ongoing experience. Only the method of science countenances an 'external permanency' – something upon which 'our thinking has no effect' (CP, 5.384) – to which our beliefs are answerable. In other words, what distinguishes the method of science from the others is that it adopts as a regulative assumption of inquiry the *Hypothesis of Reality*:

> There are Real things, whose characters are entirely independent of our opinions about them; those Reals affect our senses according to regular laws, and, though our sensations are as different as our relations to the objects, yet, by taking advantage of the laws of perception, we can ascertain by reasoning how things really and truly are; and any man, if he have sufficient experience and he reason enough about it, will be lead to the one True conclusion. (CP, 5.384)

According to the method of science, then, we cannot stabilize our beliefs by ignoring potential sources of doubt within our experience, for our beliefs are by their very nature *responsive* to experience, including recalcitrant experience.

It is important to emphasize a crucial feature of Peirce's argument in 'Fixation'. In defending the 'method of science', Peirce is *not* so much prescribing for us a new way of inquiring as he is making explicit the commitments that we already acknowledge as constitutive of proper inquiry. To see this, consider that the method of science is the only method of the four Peirce discusses that can be *self-consciously* adopted. That is, as Peirce notes, practice of the other methods leads us to doubt *the method itself* (CP, 5.384). To make the point in a slightly different way, consider that no tenacious believer *takes herself* to be practicing that method. No believer says of herself 'I am now ignoring all countervailing evidence'; rather, she says, 'I hold steadfastly to the truth, and the truth is always wholesome' (CP, 5.377). So it is with all of the nonscientific methods of inquiry – those who practice them must *take* their methods to be truth-tracking in the way that Peirce argues only the method of science can be. In other words, in order to adopt one of the nonscientific methods, one must be *mistaken* about its nature; specifically, one must *mistakenly* take one's nonscientific method to have the properties of the method of science. In this way, in 'The Fixation of Belief', Peirce is *not* trying to convince us to choose the method of science over the other methods; rather, he is trying to show us that only it conforms to what we already recognize as proper inquiry. That is, the argument of 'Fixation' is that we are already committed to the method of science and that 'we cannot help but generally adopt it' (Misak 2004a: 85).[10]

The tight connection between Peirce's pragmatic maxim and his conception of inquiry should be evident. Recall that according to Peirce, the meaning of a proposition is to be understood in terms of a subjunctive conditional of the form,

If one were to perform action A, one would observe result B.

Another way of capturing the pragmatic maxim is to say that the meaning of a proposition is to be analyzed in terms of a *hypothesis* about the results that would follow were some experiment performed. To place this in the context of Peirce's conception of inquiry, observe that, on Peirce's view, to *believe* some proposition is to be disposed to act in certain ways under a certain range of conditions. That is, to *believe* some proposition, *p*, is to take certain subjunctive conditionals to be true. Doubt ensues when our action is frustrated because experience contradicts at least one such conditional. When this happens, we inquire; that is, we try to arrive at a belief that squares with our experience and thus can guide action without engendering doubt.

Once the connection between Peirce's pragmatic maxim and his theory of inquiry is made explicit, we see that a certain view of truth emerges. Inquiry, when properly conducted, is the process of attempting to arrive at a belief that would never occasion doubt, a belief that would not give rise to recalcitrant experiences. Hence Peirce observes,

> All the followers of science are animated by a cheerful hope that the processes of investigation, if only pushed far enough, will give one certain solution to each question to which they apply it. (CP, 5.407)

Of an issue in astronomy current to his day, Peirce says of a group of scientists, 'They may at first obtain different results, but, as each perfects his method and his processes, the results are found to move steadily together toward a destined center' (CP, 5.407). Peirce continues,

> So with all scientific research. Different minds may set out with the most antagonistic views, but the progress of investigation carries them by a force outside of themselves to one and the same conclusion. (CP, 5.407)

From this follows Peirce's famous thought about truth,

> The opinion which is fated to be ultimately agreed to be all who investigate, is what we mean by truth, and the object represented in this opinion is the real. (CP, 5.407)

Due to passages such as these, Peirce is often read as advocating an 'ideal convergence' theory of truth according to which truth is to be defined as that which competent inquirers operating under ideal epistemic conditions would come to believe – what they would converge upon – once inquiry had reached its ideal limit. Such a definition of truth is curious, to say the least; more importantly, many critics have shown that it is open to a number of compelling objections. To be sure, there is a good deal of scholarly debate concerning whether in the final analysis Peirce held an *ideal convergence view of truth*. But we need not engage these questions here; they will be taken up in our chapter on truth.

Let us turn now to Dewey's theory of inquiry. Since his 1938 book, *Logic: The Theory of Inquiry* (LW12), contains his most extensive treatment of inquiry, our account will focus there.

Relatively early in the *Logic*, Dewey defines inquiry as follows:

> Inquiry is the controlled or directed transformation of an indeterminate situation into one that is so determinate in its constituent distinctions and relations as to convert the elements of the original situation into a unified whole. (LW12: 108)

There are clear echoes of Peirce in this definition. Following Peirce, Dewey sees inquiry as an activity that is engaged in *response* to a certain kind of experience, what he, again following Peirce, calls 'doubt' (LW12: 109). However, a key difference between Peirce and Dewey is already evident in the definition above. Dewey builds into his definition of inquiry the idea of a 'situation', and the corresponding distinction between 'determinate' and 'indeterminate' situations. These concepts presuppose the distinctive view of experience that Dewey develops elsewhere. His theory of inquiry is thus predicated on the correctness of that view of experience.

Yet Dewey's view of experience is philosophically weighty, and consequently highly contestable. Dewey urged that the foremost philosophical implication of the Darwinian theory of evolution was its call for the reconstruction of philosophy's traditional conception of experience. According to this traditional conception, experience is primarily the passive affair of the mind receiving impressions of external objects through the sense organs. In his 1917 'The Need for a Recovery of Philosophy' (MW10), Dewey insists that experience is 'an affair of the intercourse of a living being with its physical and social environment' (MW10: 6). A similar expression is given in *Democracy and Education*, 'when we experience something, we act upon it, we do something with it; then we suffer and undergo the consequences' (MW9: 146).

What constitutes experience on Dewey's view is not merely the sense perceptions of passive spectators on the world, but rather the dynamic participation, the continuing process of an organism's 'adjustment' (MW10: 9) not simply *to* environing conditions but *within* a social and biological environment. In the process of *experiencing*, something *happens* – an organism actively *encounters* a world within which it, if it is to continue living, must adjust.

Inquiry is on Dewey's view a particular kind of experiencing. Particularly, one conducts inquiry within and in response to what Dewey calls a 'problematic situation'. The term 'situation' is a technical term for Dewey, which he characterizes as follows:

> What is designated by the word 'situation' is *not* a single object or event or set of events. For we never experience nor form judgments about objects and events in isolation, but only in connection with a contextual whole. This latter is what is called a 'situation'. (LW12: 72; italic in the original)

The term 'situation' denotes the entire, pervasive, unique character of all conditions under which and *within* which an individual organism functions at a given time. A situation is problematic or indeterminate when its constitutive factors are in disorder.

As we have already mentioned, Dewey follows Peirce in understanding inquiry as an operation activated in response to doubt; however, unlike Peirce, Dewey understands doubt to be an 'existential' (LW12: 30) condition; that is, for Dewey, it is the *situation* that is doubtful, not simply the organism. 'Doubt' characterizes situations that are *themselves* 'uncertain, unsettled, [and] disturbed'; doubt, and presumably belief, hence are not simply states in which individual believers might find themselves, 'it is the *situation* which has these traits [such as doubt and belief]' (LW12: 109). Thus, on Dewey's view, a belief is an existential state of fitness or equilibrium between an organism and an environment. Similarly, doubt is a state of unfitness or disequilibrium. Inquiry, then, is the activity on the part of the organism of adjusting existential conditions so as to restore equilibrium.

From these considerations follows Dewey's *epistemic constructivism*, according to which 'Knowledge is related to inquiry as a product to the operations by which it is produced' (LW12: 122). Elsewhere, Dewey expresses the point in explicitly metaphysical terms,

The object of knowledge is eventual; that is, it is the outcome of directed experimental operations, instead of something in sufficient existence before the act of knowing. (LW4: 136)

According to Dewey, then, the aim of inquiry is not the discovery of an antecedent fact of the matter or state of affairs, but rather the *creation* or *construction* of a new 'situation', the bringing into being of a new object of knowledge that did not exist prior to the act of inquiry.

The precise meaning of the constructivist component of Dewey's theory of inquiry is a matter of controversy, even among his most sympathetic commentators.[11] Our aim at present is neither to evaluate Dewey's conception of inquiry in general, nor to assess his constructivism in particular. The aim is simply to emphasize that Dewey has built into his conception of inquiry an entire system of philosophical commitments. The Deweyan characterization of inquiry presupposes, at the very least, a Darwinian conception of experience as the experimental activity of an organism within an environment, an ontology of 'situations' that admit of traits such as 'determinacy' and 'doubt', and a metaphysics of objects of knowledge that emerge out of processes of inquiry. Of course, it could be that these philosophical commitments are the *correct* ones. However, the question of which are the correct metaphysical, ontological, and other philosophical commitments is surely a question that would have to be settled *by inquiry*. An account of inquiry that *presupposes* the aptness of a particular array of such commitments cannot help but beg the question in their favor. At any rate, like James, Dewey has expanded a fundamental and philosophically modest insight of Peircean pragmatism into a full-blown philosophical system whose ambitions and domain extend far beyond the more modest Peircean project of making explicit the commitments implicit in our existing practices.

CONCLUSION

According to the account we have just sketched, the philosophical progression from Peirce to James to Dewey marks a transformation of the philosophical commitments constitutive of pragmatism. What began as an intuitive methodological principle for conducting philosophical inquiry in Peirce becomes in the hands of James and Dewey a systematic philosophy in itself, complete with its own metaphysics, epistemology, and ethics. In Dewey's version, pragmatism is expanded to include in addition an aesthetic theory, a social philosophy, a philosophy of religion, a philosophy of science, and a philosophy of education. Of course, this is not to say that Peirce was not a systematic or comprehensive philosopher. In many ways, his philosophical reach extended far beyond that of James and Dewey. However, as we mentioned earlier, pragmatism is not the whole of Peirce's philosophical vision, even if it may be the center of it. To repeat, Peirce saw pragmatism as a new philosophical methodology, a way forward for philosophy. As we have seen, Peircean pragmatism is essentially the imperative to keep open the way of inquiry both by clearing away meaningless concepts and by subjecting our meaningful claims to the test of proper inquiry. Although Peirce himself spent his career documenting and systematizing the results of his own pragmatic inquiries, Peircean pragmatism in itself does not stand for any particular results of inquiry; that is, Peircean pragmatism is *not* a *Weltanschauung* (CP, 5.13). Consequently, among Peircean pragmatists there is room for disagreement over the main philosophical questions. This is not the case for Jamesian and Deweyan pragmatism, each of which tends

THE ORIGINS OF PRAGMATISM

to entail directly a particular set of philosophical answers to the standard questions.

Accordingly, the account we have proposed concurs with the spirit of Ralph Barton Perry's claim that 'the modern movement known as pragmatism is largely the result of James's misunderstanding of Peirce' (1948: 281). The account we have offered in fact goes further than Perry; it says that the pragmatisms of both James and Dewey, represent, in their own ways, radical departures from pragmatism as it was originally proposed by Peirce. On this account, pragmatism has been from the very start more than a 'vague, ambiguous, and overworked word' (Rorty 1982: 160); it has been always a deeply contested concept, and the career of pragmatism as a philosophical movement is marked more by what Richard Bernstein (1995) has called a 'conflict of narratives' than by a consensus or convergence on any philosophical idea, principle, or objective.

We hold that the conflict among pragmatists over central philosophical questions – and, indeed, over the character of pragmatism itself – is a sign of intellectual health rather than crisis.

CHAPTER 2

PRAGMATISM AND EPISTEMOLOGY

EPISTEMOLOGY

Overview

Epistemology is the systematic study of knowledge: what we know, how we know, and how we might demonstrate to others what and how we know. The modern period of European philosophy (from the seventeenth to the early nineteenth century) was marked by the centrality of such questions. René Descartes's epochal *Meditations on First Philosophy* set the stage, since in it, answering global skepticism (about the external world, truths of logic, even the thinker's own existence) is posed as the criterion for philosophical success. The answer to the global skeptic was that there had to be foundational knowledge, and the rest of our knowledge must be built up from that foundation. The difficulty, then, was to figure out what should be counted as foundational. Descartes's answer was that truths as clearly and distinctly perceived as his own existence were to serve as the foundation for knowledge. The question regularly asked was whether this foundation is broad enough to actually ground all human knowledge.

The incipient articles in the pragmatist epistemological tradition are Charles S. Peirce's 1860s methodological works, 'Questions Concerning Certain Faculties Claimed for Man', and 'Consequences of Four Incapacities'. In these articles, Peirce challenges the modern philosophical program not only on the claim that knowledge needs foundations but also on the very project of answering the global skeptic. In the place of the modern epistemology, Peirce offers a theory devoted to answering practical questions arising from human life. Inquiry, as we noted in Chapter 1, arises as a response to doubt.

PRAGMATISM AND EPISTEMOLOGY

Foundations, Peirce argues, are neither possible nor necessary, since the complete rational reconstruction of knowledge is not an issue that arises in the use and production of knowledge. Furthermore, Peirce rejects the entire skeptical problematic:

> We cannot begin with complete doubt. We must begin with all the prejudices which we actually have when we enter upon the study of philosophy . . . Hence this initial skepticism will be a mere self-deception, and not a real doubt . . . Let us not pretend to doubt in philosophy what we do not doubt in our hearts. (CP, 5.265)

There are two different ways of reading Peirce's critique of traditional epistemology. The first has it that the failure of modern epistemology portends the failure of epistemology *in toto*. We term this trajectory of pragmatism *pragmatist antiepistemology*. The second way of reading the Peircean critique sees it as calling for a reconstruction of traditional epistemological concerns in terms of the lives and interests of knowers. This trajectory we will term *pragmatist epistemology*. In this chapter, we outline a few of the defining features of traditional epistemology, present more fully Peirce's challenge to the traditional epistemological project, outline the central trends of pragmatist antiepistemology and pragmatist epistemology, and finally present what we see as the main problems for the two trends.

TRADITIONAL EPISTEMOLOGY AND PEIRCEAN FALLIBILISM

Epistemology and Pragmatism's Challenge

Epistemologists aim to describe the norms of knowledge. These norms are captured by *epistemic principles* – generalizations outlining the characteristic features of how knowledge is obtained, maintained, and demonstrated. A theory of knowledge is a collection of epistemic principles. In epistemology, it is customary to formalize these principles, and we will do so here following some standard epistemological notation. First, let us say that anyone who knows or might know something is a *subject*, and subjects are referenced with the variable S. Second, what these subjects know must be that some proposition, belief, or sentence is true, so those propositions, beliefs, and sentences will be referenced by the variables $p, q,$ and r.

27

Given this apparatus, here are some relatively noncontroversial epistemic principles:

Verity: If *S* knows that *p*, then *p* is true.

If it's false that Bill Clinton is the ruler of Mars, then no one can know that Bill Clinton is the ruler of Mars. You can't know what ain't so. But note: Not any old truth will do. You must have some *commitment* to this truth. Hence:

Commitment: If *S* knows that *p*, then *S* is committed to *p*'s truth (or *S* believes that *p*).

If you do not have any beliefs about who is the current president of France, then you do not know who the president is. Knowledge requires that you are committed to the truth of what is known. Note further that believing something that just happens to be true is not yet knowledge, either. You could have guessed luckily or have acquired the belief by some bad habit. Knowledge requires that we are not only right about what we know, but that we also know on the basis of good reasons. So,

Justification: If *S* knows that *p*, then *S* must believe that *p* on the basis of some good reason for *p*.

Knowledge is a success term, then, on two fronts. First, with knowledge, we have the truth. Second, we, in obtaining that knowledge, have expressed our rationality.

A number of serious questions emerge. What is truth? What is a belief? What is a good reason? We will have to table the discussions of the nature of truth and belief until the next chapter. Here we will pursue the central epistemological question of what it takes for a reason to be one that confers knowledge.

Skepticism plays a central role in traditional epistemology, since a natural answer to the question as to what constitutes a good reason is that a good reason is one that cannot be doubted. Descartes's project, again, was to reconstruct human knowledge from a foundation of indubitable beliefs, and this same general outline for epistemology dominated modern philosophy in both the analysis of knowledge and in the search for proper philosophical method. One of the basic thoughts behind the project was that until one had laid the foundation for knowledge, no other inquiry could proceed intelligently. Call this general epistemological and philosophical view *foundationalism*. Peirce's challenge to foundationalism runs as follows: If someone were to answer the question of what constitutes a good reason, that answer itself should be based on good reasons. Those reasons should be held on the basis of further good reasons. And so on. It seems, then, that assessing good reasons requires good reasons, and such a thought quickly puts us on the road to a series of reasons about reasons on to infinity. This is called the *regress problem*. Peirce notes the problem; he at first acknowledges that it seems we are in need of foundational first reasons:

> It would seem that there is or has been; for since we are in possession of cognitions which are determined by previous ones and these by cognitions earlier still, there must have been a *first* in the series or else our state of cognition at anytime is completely determined according to logical laws, or by our state at a previous time. (CP, 5.259)

What would define such foundational first cognitions, Peirce claims, is their cognitive independence, their immediacy. Such thoughts would be *intuitive*. However – and here is where Peirce breaks with the traditional model – such thoughts are not possible, since if some subject (*S*) were to have an intuition, that intuition would be intuitive for *S* as itself being intuitive. However, no thought can be on its own, since all thoughts are meaningful in terms of their relation to other thoughts. Peirce contends:

> [A]ll the cognitive faculties we know of are relative, and consequently their products are relations. But a cognition of a relation is determined by previous cognitions. No cognition not determined by a previous cognition can be known. It [intuition] does not exist, then, first because it is absolutely incognizable, and second because cognition exists insofar as it is known. (CP, 5.262)

The consequence is that there are no foundations for reasons because the quality of a reason is determined by the reasons supporting it.

This leads to a curious outcome: the view emerging from Peirce's criticism of foundationalism is *infinitism*. On the infinitist view, since everything can be questioned, the quest for knowledge is a never-ending process of answering questions and opening new ones. Furthermore, Peirce's view entails that one need not address the ultimate questions before proceeding with inquiry regarding nonultimate issues. That is, one does not have to refute the global skeptic before one inquires whether or not the stove is hot. Requirements that one must address the skeptic before addressing less fancy questions brings inquiring about truths to a halt, which is what Peirce takes to run afoul of one of the deepest norms of cognitive life, *The First Rule of Reason*:

Do not block the road of inquiry. (CP, 1.135)

Since we hold the results of inquiry as open to question, we are open to revising them when new information comes in, and this means that we may pursue our researches piecemeal and fit them together and bring them into equilibrium as we go. What is necessary, then, for those seeking knowledge is not an inclination to find unshakable theses, but an openness to criticism, a willingness to change one's mind, and the attitude that any one purportedly known truth could be false. Such an attitude is broadly termed *fallibilism*, and our assessment of knowledge and the reasons constituting it should be reconstructed in light of such fallibilist principles.

PRAGMATIST ANTIEPISTEMOLOGY

Three Theses of Antiepistemology

In the wake of Peirce's criticism of the traditional epistemological project, many pragmatists have taken it that epistemology in general is futile. If there are no foundations and if fallibilism is the right attitude toward knowledge, then how exactly could a reconstruction of epistemic principles take place? Put otherwise, if in order to know, one need not address the question of what constitutes knowledge or the question of what the ultimate objects of knowledge are, then those sorts of traditional epistemological projects are worthless. Pragmatism's antiepistemological trajectory is posited on a collection of three substantive philosophical views concerning knowledge and the philosophical futility of further clarification and refinement of its pursuit. They are:

Relativism: The case for any standard of knowledge cannot avoid begging the question, and hence, no standard of knowledge is privileged.

Historicism: Standards of knowledge and justification are socially and historically dependent.

Anticognitivism: Truth is not the goal of inquiry.

In this section, we present these theses. We start with relativism. Relativism begins from the observation that there is a variety of views about what we know, what are good reasons, and how to even address basic issues in crucially appraising claims to knowledge. From this, the relativist concludes that none of these views is better than any other. To illustrate this, let there be two epistemological theories, E1 and E2, each comprised of a set of epistemic principles and arguments for those principles. Epistemologists committed to E1 may say of E2 that many of its principles are wrong, and those committed to E2 may say the same of E1. As a consequence, these epistemologists have a good deal they disagree about. The question is how they might resolve their disagreement. Those committed to E1 may give their reasons, but their reasons will be drawn from the principles of good reasoning embodied by E1. But from the perspective of those committed to E2, surely these arguments would cut no ice, since the initial disagreement would be recapitulated at the level of the premises for the arguments, and those disagreements would eventually amount to full-scale strife between the respective systems. Ultimately, the anti-epistemologist reasons, those on both sides have a choice: either they dogmatically remain committed to the superiority of their own epistemological theories or they recognize that there is no nonquestion begging articulation of the proper rules for reasoning, and they give up their parochial divisions for relativism.

In these circumstances, the case for historicism is easy to make. Given that there is no privileged epistemology, the reasons any epistemologist can give for why she is committed to some principles and not others cannot themselves be because they are the sole correct principles. Instead, the explanation will be that she is committed to the principles and not others because of her social, cultural, and historical context. Those committed to E1 may be so because of some enculturation of their class and those committed to E2 may be so because of their religious upbringings and inclinations. Epistemic principles, then, are recapitulations of the social and cultural norms predominant in a historical period. Epistemology is politics writ in the language of critical reasoning.

Historicism and relativism, then, entail that inquiry as the employment of reasons to resolve disputes, disagreements, and questions, is not directed at a truth independent of inquirers. Instead, the employment of reason is a political act of reducing conflict, creating consensus, and allaying mistrust between rivals. Truth is not the goal of our researches, but instead a kind of intellectual, personal, and political stability. Anticognitivism in antiepistemology is a natural outgrowth of relativism and historicism.

The pragmatist tradition of antiepistemology holds to the tight connection between the three theses of relativism, historicism, and anticognitivism. John Dewey's attitudes toward what he calls 'the epistemology industry' (EW5: 19) are exemplary. Dewey makes the case that the impetus to the epistemologies of certainty from the Greeks to the Modern period were not purely theoretical inclinations, but rather an 'emotional substitute' for a life and world subject to vicissitudes and disappointment (LW4: 26). Epistemologies are designed to meet our needs, thus:

> One might even go so far as to say that there are as many kinds of valid knowledge as there are conclusions wherein distinctive operations have been employed to solve problems set by antecedently experienced situations. (LW4: 157)

What arises is a constructivist historicism regarding epistemic theories, one that traces epistemologies to the problematic situations they were designed to address. Given that they are all designed to solve different problems, there is no answer as to which theory is correct. Further, there is no answer as to which versions of knowledge yielded by the epistemologies approach truth. In fact, truth as a connection with an independent reality, as traditionally conceived, has dropped out of the estimations of knowledge altogether. Dewey notes:

> The glorification of knowledge as the exclusive avenue of access to the real is not going to give way soon nor all at once. But it can hardly endure indefinitely. (LW4: 237)

The upshot is that once we understand the relativist and historicist points about knowledge, even the pursuit of the real in the form of knowledge is displaced. Epistemology, then, is simply not worth doing. Richard Rorty has deepened and extended Dewey's criticism of epistemology. Rorty's early work is committed to showing that philosophy's obsession with method, with refining our approaches to the real, suffers from the permanent problem of relativism:

> To know what method to adopt, one must already have arrived at some metaphysical and some epistemological conclusions. If one attempts to defend these conclusions by the use of one's chosen method, one is open to a charge of circularity. If one does not defend them, maintaining that given these conclusions, the need to adopt the chosen method follows, one is open to the charge that the chosen method is inadequate, for it cannot be used to establish the crucial metaphysical and epistemological theses that are in dispute . . . Attempts to substitute knowledge for opinion are constantly thwarted by the fact that what *counts* as philosophical knowledge seems itself to be a matter of opinion. (1967: 1–2; italic in the original).

In a similar vein of criticism of epistemological theories out to account for and adjudicate various standards of reasoning and their connection with truth, Kai Nielson notes:

> None of these inquiries . . . puts us in greater touch with reality. We cannot determine something like that for we do not know what we are talking about in talking about reality *full stop* and we have no non-question begging criteria for determining which (if any) of the various realities we are talking about is the *really real*. (2007: 142; italic in the original)

Nielson and Rorty's central case is that any claim to know or have a reason or system of reasons must itself have a story as to how it indicates the truth better than its competitors. However, the reasons justifying this commitment will come from the greater system, which is something any system can do on its own behalf. As a consequence, to judge one system (E1) better than another (E2) by E1's standards is in the end arbitrary and intellectually vicious. The reasons one should give for preferring one system to another is the current cultural role it plays – epistemology should then give way to culture criticism. Hence Rorty says,

> It does not matter which description one uses, as long as it is clear that the issue is one about whether philosophy should try to find natural starting-points which are distinct from cultural traditions, or whether all philosophy should do is compare and contrast cultural traditions. (1982: xxxvii)

Philosophical projects designed to take on the foundationalist epistemic project to reason from indubitable premises are committed to a vision of philosophy properly construed as 'Philosophy' (with a big P), engaged in an enterprise more like playing God or at least emulating Him with one's aspirations to have one's title and one's enterprises all capitalized. (It is surprising how much one can communicate and impugn simply with *typography*.) In its stead, Rorty proposes (little-p) 'philosophy', as a project of constructing and comparing vocabularies that help us cope with the world and problems in it. On this view, epistemologies are merely the articulations of the preferred vocabularies. Each thinker and group has a vocabulary that renders the rules, and that vocabulary is *final* for that group – it is the vocabulary all the other thoughts of the group get weighed by. Rorty writes,

> All human beings carry about a set of words which they employ to justify their actions, their beliefs, and their lives. These are words in which we formulate the praise of our friends and contempt for our enemies, our long-term projects, our deepest self-doubts and our highest hopes . . . I shall call these words a person's 'final vocabulary'. It is 'final' in the sense that if doubt is cast on the worth of these words, their user has no noncircular argumentative recourse . . . beyond them there is only helpless passivity or a resort to force. (1989: 73)

But there are many final vocabularies. Consequently, we have no neutral vocabulary to adjudge which should be the absolutely final vocabulary. For each group there is a final vocabulary, but there is not a final vocabulary for all the various groups. Thus, Rorty holds that the features of knowledge are inscribed by our linguistic communities:

> [T]here are no constraints on inquiry save conversational ones – no wholesale constraints derived from the nature of beliefs, or of the mind, or of language, but only those retail constraints provided by the remarks of our fellow-inquirers. (1982: 165)

What it is to know has been reconstructed such that the objects of knowledge are no longer facts independent of human interest or agency, but features of our environment that help or hurt our endeavors and the commitments of those with whom we must cooperate. But knowledge has a deep association with objectivity, which does not seem to be itself social. What is required, then, is a reconstruction of the notion of objectivity. On the antiepistemological pragmatist model, objective knowledge is a social accomplishment and something that is more properly expressed in institutional terms. Rorty notes:

> For pragmatists, the desire for objectivity is not the desire to escape the limitations of one's community, but simply the desire to extend the reference of 'us' as far as we can. (1991: 23)

According to Rorty, the modern foundationalist model of knowledge is not only wrong about the varied cases of knowledge, but it is also wrong about the social features of knowledge, its meaning for a community of people with various needs, disagreements, and shared projects. On this point, Nielson lists the central theses of pragmatist antiepistemology:

> (1) We do not think that some arguments are *intrinsically* better than others. Justification is always to a reasonably determinate audience for a reasonably determinate purpose and is always time and place dependent; (2) there is no *natural order of reasons*; (3) there is nothing more immutable about our present ways of doing and viewing things than our past ways; (4) truth is not the goal of inquiry; (5) there are no interest-free and context-free criteria for unity, coherence, and completeness. (2007: 124; italics in the original)

Because knowledge is a function of and implicated in the lives of knowers, it reflects their interests and is a tool in the pursuit of the things important to them. The antiepistemologist reasons that there can be no universal epistemology since there is a variety of lives and a multiplicity of values. The epistemological project of taking a set of epistemic principles to be better than others, then, is either a form of parochial dogmatism or a refusal to recognize the plural values in human life.

The injunction to antiepistemology, consequently, is not simply philosophical, but political and ethical. The antiepistemologist contends that the modern framework for the analysis of knowledge renders knowing vacuous and irrelevant to the proper role of knowledge in people's lives. Dewey's metaphor of an 'epistemology industry' in philosophy, then, has a unique critical edge to it. Epistemology, though professionally organized and technically refined, is nevertheless a form of pointless busy-ness that threatens to displace genuinely important enterprises.

CHALLENGES TO PRAGMATIST ANTIEPISTEMOLOGY

Problems for Relativist Epistemology

Note, however, that the case for antiepistemology is itself an *epistemological* argument. It says that no case for an epistemic principle can avoid begging the question, so adopting relativism is the only justified response. Surely the argument presupposes an epistemic principle according to which question-begging arguments do not yield justification. Given that this rule is employed in regulating relations between rival epistemologies, the noncircularity requirement is systematic. If someone were to reject the requirement of not begging the question and argue that epistemic system E1 is better than all competitors on the basis of E1's principles, that person would simply be a dogmatic enthusiast for the view over others, not a successful advocate. The argument for relativism presupposes that there is, indeed, a nonrelative epistemic norm; the argument's conclusion is that adopting relativism is a *nonlocal epistemic success* and those who do not adopt it are *failures*. The case for relativism is thus posited on an assumption of its own falsity.[1]

Problems for Historicism

One may concede that many cases of knowledge are dependent on the activities and cooperation between people without saying that knowledge itself is a social construction. Many cases of knowledge are the result of the directed collaborations between many inquirers, and moreover, that collaboration may not have been possible without a number of political, economic, linguistic, and environmental factors coinciding. These background facts and values undoubtedly influence how inquirers reason together and what they reason about. It is socially contingent as to whether we are curious about and capable of inquiring with regard to dinosaurs and stars. This much is clear, but it is equally clear that it is not *socially* contingent whether there were dinosaurs or that a star has such and such a size. The evidence for these facts depends on the facts. That is what *evidence* is. Whether we pay attention to it and what we may do with it are all social facts, but what those facts are is not a social fact. If we fail to respect this distinction, we fail to actually pay attention to the facts we purportedly know. Dinosaurs lived long before there were humans to be interested in them, and stars are so far away that our linguistic conventions do not influence them. Taking knowledge of the world to be merely social renders the knowledge it purportedly explains utterly empty and insipid.

The upshot is that there are good ways to distinguish between epistemic systems. From our points earlier, epistemic theories that are not self-defeating and ones that allow knowledge to have the content it must have in order to be knowledge at all certainly do better than ones that do not. The fact that epistemology can be done poorly is evidence that it can be done well.

It is easy to devise a catalogue of other properties one epistemic system may have that would make it preferable to another. Consider a rough and ready list: a requirement of the publicity or shareability of reasons (no knowledge is in principle secret, or that one can always show one's work), a history of synthesizing the successful norms of other systems (intellectual cosmopolitanism), and little tolerance for contradiction within the system (consistency). Note from our first two requirements that the pragmatist conceptions of epistemology generally take knowledge to have a social character. The crucial thing is not to allow this social element of knowledge to entail that knowledge and its norms are merely social artifacts, things, as all too often is claimed, that are *socially constructed*.[2]

The antiepistemological pragmatist political outlook on knowledge entails the view that there are no privileged epistemic positions. But surely this cannot be correct – one is in a better position with regard to the content of a book if one has read it than if one hasn't. One is in a better position with regard to some historical fact if one does some research than if one merely lets one's imagination take the lead. It's better to have a proof for a mathematical formula than to have it supported by the say-so of a Magic 8 ball. These better and worse reasons are surely sorted by us as a community of inquirers, but they are sorted as they are not because of the arbitrary norms of our society, but because we recognize some are better than others. If we fail to respect that when we do (or refuse to do) epistemology, we fail to take these cases of knowledge as being cases of *knowing something*, as opposed to having one's friends let one get away with saying something or having a convenient commitment run one's life. Antiepistemology, in trying to save knowledge from the traditional epistemologist, ruins it.

Problems for Anticognitivism

Finally, the commitment to the classical epistemological project is not by necessity a futile or irrelevant endeavor. Precisely because when we do the social work of correcting or endorsing the reasons given by others, we do so not for the sake of merely reinforcing our idiosyncratic social norms or exercising some power over the corrected person, but because we are trying to get something right. The act of correction regards the evidence, and the cultural-political elements of the debates are defined by what those assessments of the evidence amount to. If we were to take the antiepistemologist seriously here, then all corrections of others would be a form of manipulation or coercion instead of truth-telling. That is, if one were to take on the attitude that all good reasons amounted to were what others recognized as good reasons (or, again, the truth is what your friends let you get away with saying), then the objective is simply that of getting away with saying things. Susan Haack has termed such an attitude intellectual 'cynicism' (1993: 193).

To see knowledge from the antiepistemologist's perspective is to see it perpetually in scare quotes: all knowledge is merely 'knowledge', or what *passes for* it.[3] As such, it seems that antiepistemologists could never really think anyone ever really *knows* anything. However, when we converse with someone with regard to some question, we do so to get it right; we do not tolerate those who lie, hyperbolize, embellish, dissemble, or unqualifiedly speculate. We value truthfulness, reliability, coherence, experience, and clear reasoning. Accordingly, when we say someone knows, we don't say she (merely) 'knows'. In short, Rorty may be right that inquiry is constrained by conversational norms, but those conversational norms are themselves epistemological norms.

PRAGMATIST EPISTEMOLOGY

Three Theses of Pragmatist Epistemology

Some hold that pragmatism is not a rejection of the epistemological project but a reconstruction of the theory of knowledge in light of the limitations and interests of knowers. Knowledge is itself a good thing – with it we not only have the truth, but we have also expressed our rationality in acquiring the knowledge. Knowledge also brings along with it other benefits – with knowledge, we relieve our ignorance, we understand, and as a result, we have solutions to problems. An account of knowledge must provide an account of these goods in addition to offering an analysis of *S knows that p*. Pragmatism's positive epistemological trajectory is posited on three substantive theses about knowledge:

Antifoundationalism: Knowledge neither has nor requires foundations.

Fallibilism: All beliefs are open to rational revision.

Instrumentalism: Knowledge and the quality of one's reasons depends on one's interests.

We will critically present the case for these three theses and then, in the next section, turn to some concerns anyone holding these commitments must answer.

Recall that the problem traditional foundationalism was supposed to solve is the regress problem. The traditional account held that there are three options for the structure of reasons: either they go in a circle, stop with some beliefs, or go on to infinity. Circles are question-begging, and giving reasons to infinity hardly seems possible for finite creatures. That leaves us with the view that there must be reasons that one may have without further reasons.

The sources for these reasons were traditionally considered dual: experience and reason. Experience provides a foundation for empirical beliefs (e.g., this is my hand, that dog is brown, I have a headache, etc.), and reason provides what is called an a priori foundation for the truths of reason (e.g., $2 + 2 = 4$; if Sam is a bachelor, Sam is unmarried; if object X has properties Q and R, object x has property Q). The question, though, was not *whether* we know these things, but *how* we do. Foundationalism is not yet a complete answer.

Experiences provide reasons for us to believe things, but only because we know how to intelligently respond to them, interpret them, see their relevance. The reasons experience provides, then, come by our *reasoning about* experience. The same goes for truths of reason. Reason itself may provide independent reasons, but these function in the way they do only because we have the understanding we do of the concepts we use. However, our understandings of those concepts are themselves composed of reasoning. For example, if someone questioned whether $2 + 2 = 4$, we could still reason our way to the answer, instead of just saying that this person just missed the boat. The consequence, then, is that what *seemed* foundational at the outset is in fact the result of a good deal of unnoticed cognitive architecture.

Additionally, foundationalism faces a dilemma, posed first by Wilfrid Sellars (1997/1956) and later advanced by Donald Davidson (1986), John McDowell (1994), and Robert Brandom (1994). The dilemma runs that if a belief (B) is held independently of other beliefs on the basis of some experience, then that experience must provide reason to hold that B is true. The experience itself, then, must either be a belief or not. If the experience is not a belief, but something different, like a state of being appeared to, then it is unclear how it can provide a reason to believe B. This is because if something is a reason to hold B true, it must function as a *premise* in an *argument* for B. But if experience is not a belief or something sufficiently like one so it can function as a premise in an argument, then the experience cannot be a reason to hold B. However, if the experience is a belief, then it certainly may function as a premise in the argument for B, but it itself is in need of justification. Either way experience cannot provide an independent foundation for knowledge.

Peirce's epistemic infinitism was the first pragmatist answer to the quandary as to how one may know in the face of the regress of reasons: inquiry proceeds infinitely, there is no end to the asking and answering of questions. Accordingly, any of our most favored theories and carefully reasoned commitments to facts may turn out to be wrong. Some new piece of evidence may turn up to upset the apple cart, someone may ask a question that requires the total revision of the way we see things. We are sure of things now, and we may justifiably be committed to our beliefs, given our intellectual resources, but we do not know where inquiry will take us and how the world will be reconceived in those new lights. Thus, Peirce holds *the end of inquiry* as a regulative ideal for fallibilist knowers:

> Truth is that accordance of the abstract statement with the ideal limit toward which endless investigation would tend to bring scientific beliefs. (CP, 5.565)

Since we are not yet at the end of inquiry, we may not yet take our current theories and arguments to be the end of the discussion with regard to the matter. Instead, we may take it that, if we've conducted our researches correctly, and if we have given those who disagree with us the space to articulate their objections, and if we have answered them all, then we may hold to our beliefs.

However, on the Peircean account, the attitude one takes toward one's beliefs as a whole is changed. Beliefs function as a *cognitive system*, one that can be tinkered with in order to function better in one area at one time, and, when circumstances change, torn down and rebuilt at another time. Willard van Orman Quine concluded that the fallibilist outlook entailed that

> Any statement can be held true come what may, if we make drastic enough adjustments elsewhere in the system . . . Conversely, by the same token, no statement is immune to revision. (1953: 43)

The rationality of a system of beliefs that constitutes knowledge, then, is not to be thought of in terms of how it is *built* (e.g., on foundations), but how it is *managed*. Wilfrid Sellars captures the thought as follows:

> [K]nowledge, like its sophisticated extension, science, is rational, not because it has a *foundation* but because it is a self-correcting enterprise which can put any claim in jeopardy, though not all at once. (1997/1956: 79; italics in the original)

The question, though, is how this self-correction and revision is possible. If reasons and inquiry have no definite stopping points and if having the truth requires the completion of such reasoning and inquiry, then how can we rationally believe anything? Or, for that matter, how can we rationally change our minds? This systematic view of one's beliefs and their rational management is that maintaining a *reflective equilibrium*, where one's experiences, intuitions, theories, and experiments all fit together in a coherent fashion.[4] The questions are (a) how one maintains such equilibrium and (b) how one can change one's mind when the equilibrium is upset.

A promising answer is that there are reasons such that, if there are no current objections or clear counterexamples to them, they may be *plausibly held*. The case for plausible reasons is, first, that life is simply too short to do infinite inquiry for every belief. If you can trace out some reasons nobody has any serious problems with, you've done pretty well. To manage much more information than that for all your beliefs is to flirt with stopping everything else in your life to keep your p's and q's straight. There seems to be a pragmatic policy of cognitive practice that reflects on the one hand our commitment to good reasons and on the other hand all the other things we want to accomplish in life. Presumptive or plausible reasons provide a surrogate for the best possible reasons on the final truth of the matter, and so long as we do not hold them as though they were irrefutable in the face of criticism or counterevidence, it seems reasonable for us to have them and operate on the basis of them. As Nicholas Rescher notes, presumption is the epistemic analogue of 'innocent until proven guilty' (2001: 28). Call the view that beliefs may be rationally held on plausible reasons *presumptivism*.

Presumptions and plausible reasons are commitments one may provisionally hold true. However, when evidence runs against them, we are obliged to forego them. Presumptive reasoning, then, is a unique and noninfinitist way of responding to the regress problem. However, presumptions themselves are indexed to shared attitudes and inclinations of coinquirers. This stands in contrast with the aspirations of universal nonrevisable reasons with classical foundationalism in Descartes's fashion. Rescher argues that on this view, an inquirer

> sees the regress as terminating in a self-supportive set of values. These values admit of alternatives all right, but these alternatives are not available *to us* . . . because we stand precommitted to the orientation at issue. (1985: 142; italic in the original)

Presumptivism, then, has a strong similarity to historicism (a commitment of antiepistemology); however, the presumptivist takes it that a discussion between one's preferred views and the alternatives is possible and pressing, while the historicist takes it that the exchange is impossible.

Robert Brandom has termed the public exchange of reasons in light of the fact of presumption, 'the default and challenge structure of entitlement' (1994: 204). The basic outline for the default element of the structure of entitlement is that beliefs held on the basis of what are generally considered reliable sources, or in line with shared values, are held presumptively. They have default status. However, because presumptions may be held only in an absence of objections, one may dislodge a group's default commitments by challenging them. By this, those for whom the belief was presumptively true must now answer for the belief, and arguments must be given. As a consequence, we may live on the basis of presumptions, but we are never slaves to them, since we may challenge their default status, and thereby revise our commitments. Our reasons not only reflect our presumptions, but they also answer to our worries and questions. This, Brandom holds, yields a 'rationalist pragmatism' (2001: 11).

The strength and quality of those reasons vary depending on what we take ourselves to know. If something is not particularly important, say, whether or not there are squirrels on campus at some Midwestern university (we presume this is not a proposition of great import except to grounds people at these universities and perhaps the squirrels themselves), then only weak plausible reasons suffice for reasonably holding the belief. Perhaps the plausible reasons would run: the Midwest is full of squirrels, especially in nonindustrial areas. Most Midwestern universities are nonindustrial, so there are probably squirrels on campus. Given how little (or nothing) hangs on the question about squirrels, just a bit of presumptive reasoning is enough to solve the quandary and we leave it at that. But now imagine that the question was made very important – perhaps because squirrel populations are indicators of the presence of some terrible virus affecting philosophers. The virus wipes out squirrel populations and then goes to the resident philosophers on campus. Now the question is very important, and presumptive reasons aren't enough to go on. In fact, we would be positively negligent if we didn't get better numbers and proof about the squirrels before we said anything about them. So, then, presumptive reasons may function as good reasons only if they have not been directly challenged or if they are evidence for only marginally important theses. When challenges arise or when the stakes rise, the quality of our reasons must rise, too.

This relation between the quality of our reasons and the values at stake is established by the fact that knowledge is integrated in our lives. It is an instrument by way of which we alleviate suffering, solve problems, and foresee difficulties. Additionally, knowledge in these matters is something that we may and often must act on. The utility of our knowledge claims, then, depends on what interests we have, what dangers await, and what values must be maintained. Because knowledge is part of our lives as interested agents in the world, the standards for knowledge vary with what is at stake in our actions implicated with that knowledge. If one says she knows that *p*, she is willing to act on it. Again, on the question about squirrels, we would say in the low stakes circumstance we know there are squirrels on campus by presumptive reasons. But in the high stakes case we would not, and this is because knowledge-attribution depends on the instrumental features of knowledge – what uses it will be put to. In low stakes, there are no important uses, and in high stakes, there are. So if in the high stakes case we *presume* there are squirrels on campus at some Midwestern university, we may unreasonably put a philosophy department in danger. The consequence, then, is instrumentalism for knowledge: the standards for a knower's evidence rise or fall proportionately to stakes for what is known, so the higher the stakes the higher the standards.

CHALLENGES TO PRAGMATIST EPISTEMOLOGY

Problems for Antifoundationalism

Pragmatist antifoundationalism requires the success either of epistemic infinitism or epistemic plausibilism. Infinitist antifoundationalism has its appeal in being an aspirational theory of knowledge. One's knowledge is always unfinished, and though one must strive for its completion, that completion is an infinite task. Surely this is correct about the growth of knowledge in general, but the question is how one can establish anything at all if there are no sources of reasons that themselves are not beholden to our other commitments. Infinitism has no positive epistemic component – there is no room for information to come into a cognitive system. The system itself is a series of nonterminating chains of inferences. But inference is a means of *transferring* justification: an argument may have a valid form, but it is still only as good as its premises. How does truth get into the system to begin with? It cannot come from more valid inferences, as they are only mechanisms of transmission. Infinitism hence suffers from a detachment from reality, since the quality of a reason is determined by reasons in its favor, there is nothing beyond the looming infinite chain of reasons to tell the difference between any nonterminating series of reasons (perhaps even random propositions stipulated to come in such an inferential chain) and one that indicates what is true. Consider two different nonterminating series of reasons, R1 and R2, with R1 supporting p and R2 supporting p's negation. What resources would reasoners have to rationally decide between them? Since the complete story for either's justification is infinitely postponed, there is no way of deciding. But infinitism is supposed to be an analysis of how to solve such problems. Peirce holds that his infinitism places his theory of knowledge amongst the problems of lived knowing. Yet, infinitism can never provide anything but *conditional reasons* for knowledge, and this problem of detachment reveals that even the conditional claims to knowledge themselves are not supported. If infinitism is to make any sense of knowledge or inquiry, then it must also entail an account of how information about the world gets into cognitive systems in a way that gives reasoners the means of telling chains of reasons indicating the truth from ones that do not. Otherwise, infinitism is an incomplete epistemic theory.

The solution for infinitism is to allow independent reasons to function alongside infinite series of inferences. Presumptive reasons could easily perform this function, and with their tentative and challengeable claims, they are always open to the further unfolding of reasons as infinitism requires. Infinitism and plausibilist epistemology, are a perfect fit. The former is an ideal picture of the whole of reasons that must be marshaled for the complete justification for any commitment, and the latter is a practical picture of the reasons that must be marshaled for the justification we need to act and convince those who need convincing. Infinitist and plausibilist fallibilism seem to be different aspects of the same overall architecture of knowledge (Fantl 2003; Aikin 2005).

The problem is that plausibilism, though it may answer the incompleteness problem for infinitism, *is itself incomplete* in precisely the same fashion. What explains the default status of the presumptively true propositions? Cognitive systems must maintain reflective equilibrium, but in what way may information come into the system so that change is required? Either the status of some reason is intrinsic to the commitment or is dependent on the commitment's public assessments.

Sellars, Rescher, and Brandom hold the latter and take it that default status for reasons is a matter of intersubjective agreement. On this view, knowledge's social element is a determinative factor with justifying reasons. Sellars holds that the presumptive status of presumptively true reports depends on their acceptability to other language users:

> A report can be correct as an instance of a general mode of behavior which, in a given linguistic community, it is reasonable to sanction and support. (1997/1956: 74)

Similarly, Rescher argues that presumptive status is a consequence of deliberations of intellectual utility and simplicity arising from the complex struggle of reasoning with others (2001: 29). That is, presumptions arise because it is often costly to challenge some commitments or because there are no viable alternatives. Brandom holds that the intellectual default status of some reports or commitments depends on group assessment as true or produced reliably:

> [W]e need not assume that the only way a believer can come to be entitled to a propositionally contentful commitment is by being able to offer an inferential justification for it. Instead, entitlement may be attributed on the basis of an assessment of the reliability of the process that resulted in the commitment being undertaken. (2001: 118; cf. 1994: 204)

The reasons one gives for a commitment can only go so far. Eventually, reason-giving between members of an intellectual community comes to a point where they either share the reasons and no longer have to argue or they defer to the reliability of one speaker or another regarding an issue. This deferential treatment of some speakers as reliable yields presumptive truth for their claims. But, from the perspective of the speakers, the question is why *these* presumptions and not *others?*

Nobody seems to disagree that our experiences give us reason to believe things about the world, and this is a presumptive empiricist–pragmatist default. However, it may be a default to believe on the basis of one's experiences, but what are the inputs for experience? Are their contents and our awareness of them dependent on how others see us? Let us consider Brandom's model. If S is judged by others to be a reliable reporter of green objects, it seems right that others may take S's reports that objects x, y, and z are green as plausible. But what about S? S surely is not relying on others' assessments when she is looking for green things. It may help her confidence that others trust her, but it won't help her decide whether something is green. These things appear one way or another to S, and in order for her to report that they look the way they do and for the very idea of S being a *reliable reporter* of how they look, *S needs to have access to how they look*.

Experience – not other beliefs, not the assessments of others, and not even S's deliberations about her experiences – has to be a source of reasons for S. These reasons may be plausible and infinitely challengeable, but they nevertheless are *sui generis*. Moreover, if experience is where S begins and to where S must return to again and again for data or correction, then pragmatist antifoundationalism is not quite as antifoundational as promised. Pragmatists have recognized this in various ways and have noted that experience is the source of challengeable justification and fallible information about the world. Peirce notes:

> Besides positive science can only rest on experience; and experience can never rest on absolute certainty, exactitude, necessity, or universality. (CP, 1.55)

Foundationalism does not require that the foundations be indubitable or immovable, only that they be sources of reasons that do not have to be inferred from other reasons. Experience is precisely this sort of source, and even though Peirce takes it that there are no first principles of thought or final grounds for knowledge, he nevertheless takes experience to be a unique source of information and ground for reasoning. What arises, again, is pragmatist *empiricism*.

It is important to note that our conclusion is not that infinitism and plausibilism are false; rather, we have argued that they are incomplete theories, unless they break with antifoundationalism. They are consistent with each other and in fact even complement one another, but neither provides an account of a nonarbitrary source of reasons independently of a broadly foundationalist view of justification yielded by experience. The classical pragmatist arguments against foundationalism, it seems, cannot be sustained. The challenge for contemporary epistemic pragmatism is a reconstruction of foundationalism.

Problems for Fallibilism

Pragmatism's fallibilism has an internal tension. Fallibilism is the view that any number of one's beliefs are false, and that one should run one's cognitive life in a way that one is able to find and revise those false beliefs. The case for fallibilism of this sort can be made from the following thought experiment. Imagine a historian of high standards and surpassing intelligence. She conducts her inquiries, visits all the archives, consults all the journal articles, and she does her scholarly best to get everything right. She then writes a very long, detailed book about her subject of study. She's read other detailed, well-researched books and they have all had errors. It is simply part of the profession to not only discover new truths but also to correct the false views of one's peers, and she even does so in her book. The question is whether, given the fact that every book (even the very best ones) that had come before her are error-filled, the finitude of her researches, and the possibility of inferential error in some arguments in the book, is our historian justified in holding that *every sentence in her new book is true?* Or may she hold that there is likely any number of errors in it? It seems cognitive modesty here is most reasonable. This is so for even the most advanced researchers and their books. How might our less-refined beliefs fare under such scrutiny? Fallibilism seems the right attitude.

However, what it is to have a belief is to hold it to be true. Some S's holding a proposition (p) as true means that S reasonably may use p in further arguments and inferences. So if S has beliefs that p, q, and r, then it seems S also should believe that they are collectively true, so the complex proposition (p & q & r) is true. S can do this for the entirety of her beliefs, so S may believe the very complex proposition with every one of her beliefs functioning as a conjunct:

(Φ): (p & q & r & ... & z)

The problem is that fallibilism requires that S deny Φ because any number of her beliefs is false, and if even one is false, the conjunction of all of them is false. It seems, then, we have a conflict between the logic of belief and the demands of cognitive modesty. On the one hand, if S believes p, S holds that p is true, and truths aggregate by the conjunction 'and'. From the *first person* perspective of belief, beliefs are *transparent* – if S holds to the belief that p, S simply holds that p is true. For example, if someone asks you what you believe is in your bedroom right now, you don't think about what you believe, you just think about what's in your bedroom.

On the other hand, we realize, especially with others, just because some S believes that p, it does not follow that p is true. S may *think so*, but we clearly see the difference between *her* holding that p is true and *it being true*. It turns out that with fallibilism, subjects are capable of taking on a *third person perspective* with their own beliefs.

The question is how the two attitudes can square with one another. At first blush, they are utterly inconsistent. From the first person perspective, one must view all one's beliefs as true (otherwise they wouldn't be things that count as beliefs), but from the third person perspective, there is a gulf between one's beliefs and truth such that one should take it that many of one's beliefs are likely false.

One solution is to take fallibilism as less a view one should have regarding one's beliefs but rather a *policy* or a *rule of thumb* for managing one's beliefs. The truth of fallibilism is not in one's overt belief of it, but rather it is in one's openness to correction and willingness to revise one's commitments. Call such an outlook *policy fallibilism*.

The problem with policy fallibilism is that without the commitment to the truth of the view, it is unclear how the policy is justified from the perspective of believers. If one's beliefs are true, then one shouldn't proceed to act as though some are false; instead, if they are true, you should act as though they are true. As such, policy fallibilism may reduce the contradiction between fallibilism and the logic of first person belief, but it renders acting on belief irrational.

Alternately, one may simply tolerate the inconsistency between the logic of belief and fallibilism, and perhaps even in doing so reject one of our proposed regulative requirements of cognitive rationality, namely, that of not tolerating contradictions. What is the trouble with having both the belief that all one's commitments are true and the belief that they are not? That they are inconsistent is not yet an answer, since the question now is why consistency is valuable. The key to the toleration view is to see that the two commitments shift back and forth: one sees one's beliefs at one time from the first person perspective and at another time from the third, and the circumstances determine which is appropriate. Call this outlook *perspective fallibilism*.

The problem with perspective fallibilism is that the assessments of the beliefs do not themselves amount to the beliefs being all true or not all true *from that perspective*, but true or not *full stop*. If one of them is right, the other is not. Tolerating the contradiction should first be posited on *acknowledging the contradiction* as such and not trying to evade it. An old argument against tolerating inconsistency is that if one tolerates inconsistency, such toleration must be different from *not* tolerating it. However, if one tolerates inconsistency, this difference disappears. What it is to hold that a view is right is also to hold propositions inconsistent with that view are false. Tolerating inconsistency here makes hash out of the norms of disagreement. Typically, we think that if one person believes that *p* and another person believes that *p* is false, they disagree and one must be wrong. We argue, experiment, and inquire to resolve disagreements, and the singular means of doing that is determining who is right and who is wrong. If inconsistency is tolerated, we eliminate the primary engine of inquiry.

However, the toleration of inconsistencies may not be global but restricted only to the relation between fallibilism and the logic of belief. The perspective fallibilist might say that we ought not tolerate *all* contradictions, but just *this one*. We should do so precisely because of the weight on both sides of the issue – we cannot break the stalemate. So we must make an exception. It may simply be the case that human rationality runs on inconsistent norms, and it is our fate to live with them. Nicholas Rescher frames the situation:

> Of course we stand committed to our truths; imperfect though they may be, but we have nowhere else to go. We have no alternative to proceeding on the 'working hypothesis' that . . . *our* truth is *the truth* . . . Fallibilism is our destiny. Given our nature as a creature that makes its way in the world by use of information we have to do the best we can. (2003: 36; italics in the original)

One might call such an attitude *tragic fallibilism*. But we do not have to accept such a gloomy picture just yet. Fallibilism and the logic of belief share the commitment that all belief is *full belief*, that believing that *p* is true is to hold unqualifiedly to *p*. But presumptive reasons do not justify unqualified assent, so there is with all belief a kind of conditionality, and with such conditionality, one must acknowledge the likelihood of being wrong. If belief is seen on such a graded scale, and one proportions one's commitment to the assessed quality of one's reasons, then the tension between fallibilism and the logic of belief may be mitigated.

Problems for Instrumentalism

The instrumentalist view of knowledge, the view that standards for knowledge rise or fall depending on the value of what is at stake, faces a serious puzzle formulated by Robert Howell (2005). Let us assume that Sam has a brother, Bill. They share the camaraderie that brothers do, but they live far apart. One Tuesday afternoon, Sam has the thought:

(*W*): Bill is working.

Sam is justified in believing that *W* is true on the basis of presumptive reasons: it's a Tuesday afternoon, Bill's got a job, it's not a holiday, and nothing hangs on the truth or falsity of this belief. But now imagine Sam finds himself asking another more significant question. He now wants to know whether:

(*A*): Bill is alive

This proposition, because of Sam's attachment to Bill, is very important. On the pragmatist instrumentalist theory, the stakes are higher, so the standards must go up. Presumptive reasons, then, cannot be used to answer important questions.

However, if Sam knows *W*, then it must follow that he knows *A*, because *W* entails *A*. Bill cannot be working if he's not alive. Surely Sam knows that. So since Sam does know that Bill is working, he knows Bill is alive. That's just logic.

The appeal of this reasoning is that knowledge is systematic; that is, if you know p, then p gets to function as a premise in your further reasonings about other questions. Knowledge not only settles the matter with what you know, but it also gives you the tools to figure out plenty of other things, too. Call this the *systematicity of knowledge*. All articles of knowledge are potentially relevant to other articles of knowledge. Deductive logic captures a good number of these cases of relevance. So if S knows p and S also knows that p deductively entails q, then it seems S is in a very good position to claim to know q. In fact, it seems clear we should say that, if S does the deduction, S *does* know q, otherwise it's a mystery how deductive logic is at all relevant to knowledge. Call this the *closure principle*.

If the closure principle is right, then Sam may know A on the basis of his knowledge of W. If this is right, the importance of A does not raise the standards for Sam's knowledge of W, because he knows W on the basis of presumptive reasons. It seems, then, that instrumentalism is plainly false.

But the instrumentalist has another option: because A is important and A is implicated in W, as the standards for A rise, accordingly the standards may rise for W. As a consequence, instead of *low* standards transmitting across known deductive entailments, it is *high* standards that transmit. The trouble is that now this makes presumptive knowledge virtually impossible because all cases of presumptive knowledge entail at least something important that will raise the stakes. For example, return to our earlier case with the squirrels on college campuses in the Midwest. The presumptive truth of squirrels living on campuses in the Midwest entails that animal life is possible in the Midwest. Surely this is a very significant proposition, especially to those thinking about majoring in philosophy in colleges there. We want (and indeed do have) more definitive proof of life in the Midwest than just the presumptions. But if the high standards run back to the squirrels, then we cannot know *that* by presumption, either. So if high standards run back over entailments, presumptivism is false, and by that, instrumentalism is false (since low-risk cases turn out not to be settled by low-standards reasons).

A final strategy for instrumentalism is to bite the bullet and reject the closure principle. This means holding that, despite the fact that there is a deductive logical relation between the two propositions each of different standards for justification, given the stakes, knowledge of one does not bear on the knowledge of the other. That is, given what is at stake, Sam knows W but not A, even though he knows that W entails A. Instrumentalism, then, requires the fracturing of human knowledge into interest-specific uses of the knowledge in question. Cases of knowledge, then, can have no broader implications regarding other things one might know. Deductive logic, then, transmits knowledge only if one cares equally about the premises and the conclusions. Surely this is a high price to pay for maintaining the commitment to instrumentalism, but given the arguments at this stage, it is instrumentalism's only option. Instrumentalism risks breaking the systematicity of knowledge. This certainly runs counter to the purposes and usefulness of knowledge.

It is not a good option, further, since Howell shows that it entails an absurd view of knowledge-acquisition (2005: 132–3). Let us return to Sam's questions about Bill and specifically with A. Sam, perhaps, knows of himself that when he has a drink, his cares are less urgent. So when Sam starts worrying about whether Bill is alive, Sam has a drink and calms down. After a good number of drinks, Sam doesn't have *any* cares. Given this, the stakes for Sam are lowered, so Sam now may know A on the basis of very weak plausible evidence. The solution to the problem of not knowing in a high stakes situation, then, could be to take steps to *care less* about the consequences. Once the stakes are lowered, the standards are too. In turn, *one knows more by caring less*. If instrumentalism is true, then the best solution to ignorance may be a drinking binge.[5]

CHAPTER 3

PRAGMATISM AND TRUTH

THEORIES OF TRUTH AND THEIR PREREQUISITES

Preliminaries

In the previous chapter, we introduced the epistemic principle *Verity*: if S knows that p, then p is true. Knowing is a connection between a knower and a truth. Our focus was on the knower and her reasons, and truth remained unexamined. However, it is clear that the question of truth is implicated in the questions of the nature of knowledge, so it is necessary here to wrestle with the question, 'What is truth?'

Yet pursuing a clear view of truth is not merely instrumental to our pursuit of an account of knowledge. Truth is itself intrinsically interesting and worth getting clear about. Our beliefs are things we take to be true. So we ask, What is it for our beliefs to be true? Additionally, any account of our reasoning will require that we develop logics, and a central notion of any deductive logic is that of *validity*, that the truth of the premises guarantee the truth of the conclusions. What is it for premises and conclusions to be true? How is truth something that can be *guaranteed*?

Imagine an economist developing a theory about money. If her theory is going to even have a chance of being right, the theory must either account for (or at least be consistent with) some obvious features of money: it may be exchanged for goods and services, its value is contingent on the trustworthiness of the institution that issues it, some have more of it than others, and so on. If the economist's theory entailed a denial of one or more of these commitments, we would have good reason to believe that something has gone wrong. If someone proposes a theory of money that entails that we all really have the same amount, it seems clear that the theory is either spectacularly false or is just not really a theory of *money*. The theory fails a prerequisite for being a theory worth accepting. It is important with prerequisites to keep in mind that if a theory *passes* the prerequisites, it does not follow that the theory is correct. However, if the theory *fails* the prerequisites, we can reasonably hold that it is wrong. Think of prerequisites on analogy with classes college students must take to graduate. If a student takes the required classes, it doesn't guarantee that she graduates, but if she doesn't take them, it guarantees she won't.

There are some prerequisites for a theory of truth. Trial by prerequisites is a powerful way of understanding the failure of traditional theories of truth and the aspirations of the pragmatist alternatives. There are some things we know. In light of the *Verity* principle from earlier, if someone knows that *p*, *p* is true. Additionally, if *p* is true, and some other person believed that not-*p*, that other person's belief is false. We believe that the earth revolves around the sun, and given the evidence of the sciences, we have good reason to hold it is true. Ptolmey and a good number of others were committed to the theory that the sun revolves around the earth, and that theory (if we are right) is false. So a theory of truth is constrained by the thought that the things we believe, the propositions we commit to, theories we hold, judgments we make, and so on may be evaluated according to their truth or falsity. So theories of truth, if they are going to be relevant at all to us as thinkers, are constrained by the prerequisite:

Cognitive significance: If *S* has a belief, theory, or commitment *p*, then *p* is either true or false.

The upshot is that any theory of truth must be relevant to the kind of things we hold to cognitive scrutiny, namely our beliefs, theories, and hypotheses.

We evaluate our cognitive commitments according to their truth or falsity because something hangs on such evaluations. We want true beliefs and do not want false ones. If someone says *p* is true, she says *p* is right – *p* wins her endorsement. If she says *p* is false, she is saying *p* is wrong – she rejects *p*. If you had to choose between a set of beliefs (say, about penguins) that were guaranteed to be true and another set guaranteed to be false, it seems clear that the true ones would be preferable. All things being equal, truth is preferable to falsity. So truth attribution is evaluative.

Normative significance: It is better to have true beliefs than false beliefs.

Truth is a success term. That is, when we have true beliefs, we have gotten things right, and when we have false ones, we have missed the mark (Lynch 2005). A further consideration is that when we use the term *true* in assessing beliefs and theories, we lend our assent to those theories. So saying 'It is true that Nashville is in Tennessee' is equivalent to just saying 'Nashville is in Tennessee'. So if *it is true that* 2 + 2 = 4, then 2 + 2 = 4. Moreover, if Larry was one of the Three Stooges, then *it is true that* Larry was one of the Three Stooges. Saying a proposition is true does not add anything to the proposition's content and does not do anything more than unequivocally announce endorsement of the proposition. Saying that *p is true* is just a very explicit or long-winded way of just saying *p*. So attributing truth to a proposition does not change its meaning, and as a consequence, cases of assessing a proposition as true are logically equivalent to simply holding that they obtain. We may represent the relation of logical equivalence with the biconditional *if and only if* (or *iff*). So, we have the requirement of truth:

Logical equivalence: The proposition, belief, or theory *p* is true iff *p*.

Now, given that adding *is true* to any proposition does not change its meaning or add anything to it, we can add any number of *is true* assessments to a proposition. So if it is true that *p*, it is true that it is true that *p*. We can add as many *is true* statements as we want without changing the truth of the proposition. This yields the requirement for a theory of truth (with the ellipsis standing for indefinite iterations of *is true*):

Iteration: (((*p* is true) is true) . . .) is true iff *p*.

Truth attribution, then, is *iterable*, in that we may do the same thing (add *is true* to the previous proposition) without formal constraint.

The final prerequisite for a theory of truth requires that we talk about a truth and how it is true. Consider: Nashville is in Tennessee.

So it is true that Nashville is in Tennessee. Now, since the two thoughts are equivalent, they are *logically symmetric* – it does not matter which one comes first. So if Nashville is in Tennessee, it is true that Nashville is in Tennessee. If it is true that Nashville is in Tennessee, Nashville is in Tennessee. However, the two statements are not *explanatorily symmetric*. It makes sense to say, 'It is true that Nashville is in Tennessee *because* Nashville is in Tennessee'. But it doesn't make sense to say, 'Nashville is in Tennessee *because* it is true that Nashville is in Tennessee'. Our beliefs and theories are *about the world*, and they are true or false depending on how the world is. The facts about reality make our beliefs true or false, but not the other way around. So we may say that the truth or falsity of our beliefs is in a sense explained by what they are about.

Explanation: The proposition, belief, or theory *p* is true because *p*.

We might say that our theories are true because they are right about their objects, and they are false when they are wrong about their objects. So if someone has the belief that the sun revolves around the earth, we would say her theory is false because the sun does not revolve around the earth. She has the facts about the sun wrong, and that makes her belief false.

Truth and Correspondence

One very appealing and very old theory of truth is the *correspondence theory of truth*, which holds that the truth of a proposition consists in the correspondence of a proposition and the world. So a subject's belief that the cat is on the mat is true because the belief names an object (the cat) and predicates a relational property of it (being on the mat), and it turns out that the named object is in the relation of being on the mat. There is an *isomorphism* between the proposition and the world – the names and predicates on one side map the objects and properties on the other. That's what it is to be right about the world. The belief accurately represents reality, and this success at representing reality explains the belief's truth. What makes the correspondence theory especially appealing is how it is designed especially to address the normativity and explanation prerequisites for a theory of truth. Truth is a success term because the beliefs are true by the accuracy of their representation. Beliefs aim at truth, and correspondence is what it is for beliefs to hit the mark. The way the world is explains whether or not a belief corresponds or not. On these two fronts, the correspondence theory has impeccable appeal. Correspondence, however, suffers from many difficulties. One is that *correspondence* is a vague term, and *isomorphism* and *mapping* don't clarify things as well as we may like. How is the belief that *it is wrong to lie* like a map? Another problem is that the theory requires that there are *negative facts*. If truth is explained by correspondence, falsity is explained by a failure to correspond. If p is false, then the proposition (q), *p is false*, is true. But to what does q correspond to? *The fact* that p is false? What exactly is that fact? But these are puzzles for the correspondence theory that may or may not be resolved. A more serious problem looms for the theory in the trial by the rest of the prerequisites.

The Frege Regress

On the correspondence theory, if the proposition that *the cat is on the mat* is true, then the proposition corresponds to reality. This is saying more than just that the cat is on the mat. When we say a proposition corresponds to reality, we are not only talking about reality. We are also talking about the proposition's *relation* to reality. So for it to be true that p corresponds to reality, the proposition 'p corresponds to reality' needs all the following things: the fact that p, the proposition that p, the correspondence between the two, and the correspondence between the proposition 'p corresponds to reality' and those earlier three items. Correspondence is supposed to be a simple theory. Things just got complicated.

The German logician Gottlob Frege reasoned that given the difficulty associated with truth-iterability, the problem is prohibitive of *any* substantive theory of truth:

> And any other attempt to define truth breaks down. For in a definition certain characteristics would have to be specified. And in their application to any particular case the question would always arise whether it were true that the characteristics were present. So we would be going around in a circle. So it seems likely that the content of the word 'true' is *sui generic* and indefinable. (1918–19/1997: 59)

The problem is that the correspondence theory of truth (or any other theory of truth) makes the proposition 'the proposition p is true' no longer logically equivalent to the proposition 'p' because the former must invoke things (a proposition, reality, and their correspondence) and the latter is only about one thing (reality). As a consequence, we get a proliferation of extra facts, and this shows that the correspondence theory runs afoul of the logical identity requirement. If the attribution of truth to p and the unadorned expression of p were logically equivalent, then they would invoke the same facts. This problem has been traditionally called the *Frege Regress*, and it seems that the correspondence theory of truth cannot avoid this problem.

Truth and Coherence

A further regulative thought about truths is that they not only should not contradict each other, but they also should hang together in a coherent fashion. Facts fit together, and given what we saw in the last chapter concerning the systematicity of knowledge and the closure principle, known facts can bear on one another in ways captured by our various logics and theories. The fact that the truth of a premise can guarantee the truth of a conclusion in a valid argument shows that (at least some) truths are related to each other in very deep ways. Many modern philosophers (Leibniz, Spinoza, and Hegel most prominently) developed a theory of the structure of reality based on the thought that *all* facts were connected in such deep ways. This thought is sometimes called *the doctrine of internal relations*. The central claim of the doctrine is that if something is a fact, it must *fit with* the rest of reality. That fitting with the rest of reality may make it a consequence of and also an initiator of a series of causes, it may function as evidence for some other fact, or it may prevent another fact from coming to be. An analogy may help. On this view, reality is like a big jigsaw puzzle, and facts are like pieces. The pieces must not only fit with those immediately around them, but they must all fit together in a way that makes the puzzle render an intelligible picture. One piece gone missing or put in incorrectly ruins the whole puzzle. So individual pieces must not only match up with those immediately next to them, but they must fit into the overall whole, and it is that overall whole that determines how well each piece fits.

Facts are facts, then, not just because they fit with the other facts around them, but because they *cohere* with reality as a whole. From this picture of reality we may extract a theory of truth according to which propositions are true if and only if they cohere with all true propositions. The truth or falsity of a belief is determined by its membership of a system of truths.

Just like the correspondence theory, the coherence theory has its appeal. It seems right that facts must hang together coherently. All truths should make sense, and it seems clear that we would cash this out in terms of its relevance and intelligibility in terms of the rest of things that are true. These features of *coherence* speak directly to the explanation and normativity prerequisites for a theory of truth. However, there are some questions about what *coherence* really is. It must be a relation that has more meat to it than consistency (i.e., the propositions do not contradict each other), but what? Moreover, it also seems clear to anyone who ever has read fiction that a coherent story is not necessarily a true story. In fact, given the wide variety of coherent fictional worlds from Homer's *Iliad* and Virgil's *Aeneid* to the *Star Wars* Galaxy, coherence is a very weak way of understanding truth, since there are so many coherent fantastic falsities. Further, the old saw, *Truth is stranger than fiction* is apt, since coherence regulates our fictions, but reality seems to have many things that do not seem to fit. Coherentists about truth have made a good deal of progress in addressing these puzzles, but a more serious (now familiar) problem looms for the coherence theory.

The Frege regress renders the coherence theory incoherent. Consider again the cat on the mat. If the cat is on the mat, it is true the cat is on the mat. If the coherence theory is right, the proposition *the cat is on the mat* coheres with the rest of the true propositions. So the proposition that it coheres with the rest of the true propositions must be true, and then the proposition that it coheres must itself cohere. Once again, we are off to the races. The problem is that, like the correspondence theory, the coherence theory makes statements of truth-attribution to a proposition (*it is true that p*) no longer logically equivalent to the proposition *p*. This yields a vicious regress, and as a consequence shows us that the theory runs afoul of the prerequisite of logical equivalence.

The project of analyzing and defining truth in terms of correspondence or coherence seems to not only have a number of things going for it, but it also suffers serious problems with the very idea of the project. Pragmatist theories of truth arise out of the concern that the traditional project was wrongly framed.

PEIRCEAN POSITIVISM

The Pragmatic Maxim and Its Consequences

Peirce's 'How to Make Our Ideas Clear' is the first attempt to devise a pragmatist theory of truth. Peirce's central thought was that one does not test one's theories for their truth in how they might be isomorphic with reality or whether they hang together in some compellingly coherent way, but rather, *one puts one's ideas to the test of their results*. Peirce contends that if we are to be clear about our beliefs, we must construct our theories in light of the *pragmatic maxim* (CP, 5.402). To understand what it would be for a proposition to be true is to understand how experiences would be different were that proposition false. So understanding the truth of the proposition *the cat is on the mat* is constituted by an understanding of the practical consequences of the cat being on the mat – a bowl of milk next to the mat will likely be drunk, mice will avoid the mat, one should expect howls of protest if one wipes one's feet on the mat. Truths have consequences, and to understand those truths, we must grasp the differences they make for our experience. Peirce later calls this take on truth a 'prope-positivism' (CP, 5.411).

The Peircean strategy, then, explains well the normativity of truth: true beliefs and theories help us anticipate experiences and avoid unpleasant outcomes, and they help us control matters so that we may maximize the things that are valuable. Additionally, Peirce's theory has immediate connection with the cognitive significance of truth: we now have a story to tell as to how some of our beliefs are true and some are not. Truth is relevant to our lives, it is not some theoretical posit.

Pragmatism is a brass tacks philosophy. The truth of a belief is constituted by its successful practical consequences. Given truth's role in our lives, we are not just looking for truth, but for truths that matter. Many truths, really, are cheap – we can get any number of worthless truths from reading the telephone book, or counting the number of dust specks on our desks. What pragmatism impels us to do is look for and pursue truths that are *significant* (Haack 1993: 199; Kitcher 2001: 65–8; Lynch 2004: 51).

Simply working, though, is not enough. An idea can be convenient, but there are limits to its usefulness. What Peirce is looking for is a kind of stable usefulness, a durable and reliable set of expectations. Of course, we are never sure that our current ideas will be useful tomorrow – we may have to change our minds given new evidence, and we may face new problems. In light of the fallibilist picture of knowledge outlined in the previous chapter, we cannot know beforehand which ideas will work out. However, we can know after the fact. As a consequence, the only perspective from which any specific truth may be defined in terms of usefulness in the long run is that from the *end of the long run*. Peirce writes:

> The logical warrant [for accepting a theory as true] is that this method persistently applied to the problem must in the long run produce a convergence . . . to the truth, for the truth of a theory consists largely in this, that every perceptual deduction from it is verified. (CP, 2.775)

Here Peirce seems to be endorsing enthusiastically the kind of ideal convergence theory of truth that was mentioned in Chapter 1. To be sure, Peirce scholars are eager to interpret him in ways that do not commit him to such a view (Hookway 2002; Misak 2004a); however, since it is the most common reading of Peirce, it is worth spelling out the ideal convergence interpretation and raising some of the difficulties it faces.

As we noted earlier, the ideal convergence view has consequences for and is tied with Peirce's theory of knowledge, in that the verification of every perceptual deduction of a belief is an infinite task. Since truth is a function of such an infinite task of verification, it follows that only theories held at the end of infinite inquiry are the true ones. Hence Peirce:

> The opinion which is fated to be ultimately agreed by all who investigate is what we mean by the truth. (CP, 5.407)

Thus if the community of investigators at the end of inquiry believes a proposition *p*, *p* is true. Additionally, if *p* is true, given our requirements on what it would mean for *p* to be true, *p* is what inquirers would believe at the end of. By the definition of the biconditional (*if and only if*), we may then yield a Peircean theory of truth as ideal convergence:

> *Peirce's convergence theory:* The proposition, belief, or theory *p* is true iff *p* is held at the end of inquiry.

A true belief is one that is evidentially unassailable, one to which one will never have evidence undermine it, and the criterion for this is the notion of the end of inquiry. Again, we don't know which ones of our beliefs have that status until all the evidence is in.

Challenges for the Peircean Convergence Theory

The Peircean convergence theory occasions a few puzzles. First, it seems that there are plenty of truths that are inaccessible to inquiry. For example, on the morning before he gave his famous funeral oration, the Athenian leader Pericles blinked an even number of times before breakfast or not. It is inaccessible to researchers how many times he blinked, how long his breakfast was, and whether or not there even was a breakfast. But it seems intuitive that the proposition that Pericles blinked an even number of times before breakfast is either true or false, even though it is inaccessible to historians. Call this the problem of *buried secrets*.

In one way, buried secrets shows that Peirce's theory is in tension with the explanation requirement, since the convergence theory demands we say that a proposition is true because inquirers believe it. But this seems backward. Given the explanation requirement, shouldn't we say that inquirers believe that *p* is true, because *p*? Here we see an in principle distinction between the epistemic criteria for truth and the nature of truth. Peirce's convergence theory conflates them. The explanation requirement and buried secrets are posited on the separability of truth from inquiry and knowledge – there are some truths that are not accessible and unknowable.

Consider another puzzle. On the convergence view, statements about the past are really shorthand statements about the future! On Peirce's theory, when we talk about Pericles or dinosaurs, the truth about what we are saying – *and what we are really talking about* – is experience and evidence in the future. That is, when someone says that, *Pericles blinked three times during breakfast*, this person is not saying something about the past, but is making a prediction about what inquirers will believe in the future. This seems to get things entirely upside down. Call this *the future truths about the past problem* (Fumerton 2002: 85). New work on Peirce promises to respond to these puzzles (DeWaal 1999; Misak 2004a). One could respond to buried secrets by hypothesizing more and more sensitive means of detecting truths or noting that there could always be some revelation regarding any fact (e.g., a newly unearthed papyrus about Pericles' day just before the funeral oration). However, this response invites the Frege regress. If a proposition's (p) truth is identified with the conclusions of inquirers at the end of exhaustive investigation about p, then the truth of the proposition (q) that p is true will be identified with the conclusions of inquirers with regard to how inquirers believe with regard to p. So p's truth is that inquirers believe that p. And q's truth (that p is true) will be that inquirers will believe that inquirers believe that p. So for q to be true, inquirers at the end of inquiry will not only need to have a view about p, but they will also need to have evidence about each other's beliefs and believe as a consequence that they are in agreement. Let r, then, be the belief that inquirers will believe that inquirers believe that p. For r to be true (hold on to your hats!), inquirers will have to believe that they believe that they believe that p. If truth is equated with what is believed at the end of inquiry, then attributions of truth to a proposition are no longer logically identical to the proposition. As a consequence, Peirce's theory does not pass the identity prerequisite (see Schmitt 1995: 93; Fumerton 2002: 10; Fine 2007: 55).

The theory can be salvaged, though. The crucial step in the defense is to note that Peirce's theory of meaning in terms of consequences and his theory of truth are not in the same game as the traditional theories of truth. Frege's regress poses a problem for *definitions* of truth. The lesson of the Frege regress might just be that it is a mistake to try to define truth. One might propose, then, that the Peircean theory is intended to be a tool of inquiry, not a definition of truth: we understand truth in terms of our ideal cognitive abilities, since they are things we can control and have access to. The Peircean theory aims to delineate *markers of truth* and to describe its properties relevant to the interests of those who need to find answers to questions. Thus Misak,

[Peirce] tries to get us to see the difference between two respectable tasks. The first is the provision of an analytic definition of a concept, which might be useful to someone who has never encountered the concept before. The second is the provision of a pragmatic elucidation of a concept – an account of the role of the concept plays in practical endeavors. His interest lies in the second of these tasks. (2004a: viii)

On this reading, the Peircean theory is a regulative ideal for our researches. Commitments to truth are also commitments to the success of inquiry. The Peircean theory is thus a theory of cognitive striving; it holds that in perfecting and refining the tools of argumentation and experiment, we will progressively improve our views. As such, the Peircean theory is a reconstruction of our attitudes about what a philosophical theory should be and what the proper objects of inquiry are. If it seems that conflict over a certain question is interminable because of the nature of the issue, then a better plan is to revise the debate instead of persisting in a hopeless enterprise. If consensus is impossible in light of the logic of the data, it is likely that there is no fact of the matter to be in consensus about. So it goes with truth conceived traditionally, and so we are inclined toward a Peircean revision of the project. We will return to this deflationary reading of Peirce's theory of truth in the final section of this chapter.

JAMESIAN PRAGMATISM

Truth and What Works

The lesson of the Frege regress, from a Peircean perspective, is that truth is the sort of thing one may not have a substantive theory about. Another response to the problem is to forego theorizing about truth beyond emphasizing its value for believers. William James takes this track, and he articulates truth's value in terms of how true beliefs work:

Any idea upon which we can ride, so to speak; any idea that will carry us prosperously from any one part of our experience to any other part, linking things satisfactorily, working securely, simplifying, saving labor; is true for just so much, true insofar forth true *instrumentally*. (WWJ, 382; italic in the original)

Truth, as a good, is not intelligible unless it is integrated in our lives. As Hilary Putnam notes of James's strategy with truth, 'mere resemblance never *suffices* for truth. It is what we do with our "images" that makes the difference' (1997: 172; italic in the original). As such, a true idea is not intrinsically more valuable than false ones; instead, the value of true ideas arises from their function in experience. James acknowledges the normative difference between true and false beliefs:

We ought to think the true, we ought to shun the false, imperatively. (WWJ, 442)

However, *which* truths one ought to think and *when* one actively should shun the falsities is a matter of and contingent on the vicissitudes of a human life. Truth as an abstraction is, as James calls it, 'Truth with a big T in the singular' (more philosophical work being done with typography!), but it is unclear how the abstraction is relevant to the thoughts we think. For an account of truth to bear on our cognitive attitudes, we must attend to 'concrete truths in the plural' (WWJ, 442–3). Having particular truths is preferable to falsehoods because they are more expedient in the particular situations they bear on. As a consequence, there is not much more to say about truth beyond the observation that truths arise from successful practices and useful views. The value of truth is to be articulated *instrumentally* – from that of *true beliefs*. To hold that truth has a value independent of the beliefs and their role in our lives is an empty abstraction. Again, James and Peirce view truth in terms of its consequences, but their focus is different. Peircean positivism focuses on the difference of observable consequences between the truth or falsity of a belief, on how experience would be different if *p* is true or if *p* is false. James's theory is focused on the consequences of whether the belief is held or not – how experience is different if you believe or do not believe *p*. James, presumably, takes this difference between his view and Peirce's to be one that resists the inclination to abstract truth. A Jamesian may say the *psychologizing* we noted in Chapter 1 is what makes his theory vital instead of abstract and empty.

To combat the inclination to abstract truth from the processes of lived successes that yield it, James makes an analogy. Truth is like health and wealth. Health is the name of the proper functioning of processes like digestion, circulation, sleep, and so on. So it is the same thing to say, 'He sleeps well because he is healthy', as 'He is healthy because he sleeps well'. The same with wealth – we do not prefer

'Carnegie is wealthy because of his holdings' to 'Carnegie has his holdings because he is wealthy'. Instead, we see them as equivalent – wealth and health are identical with the concrete benefits. So it goes with truth. 'Truth makes no other kind of claim and imposes no other kind of thought than health and wealth do' (WWJ, 440). There is a variety of uses and benefits true beliefs and theories yield, and there is no singular truth, but many plural truths. As a consequence, James reasons, theories of truth that take truth to be a property abstractable from those successes are bound to failure. This is why truth is not the sort of thing or property we can have a theory about.

James's strategy, then, is to maximize two of our prerequisites for truth – cognitive significance and normativity. With cognitive significance, he makes the case that truth bears on our beliefs insofar as they play a role in our lives and further, that the evaluation of truth and falsity of our beliefs comes to how well they function in our lives. So with normativity, we explain the preferability of true beliefs to false ones in terms of the preferability of their results. The implication is that traditional theories of truth fail on these accounts. Why, the Jamesian may ask rhetorically, would anyone other than a philosopher want to have or be able to tell whether he has true beliefs? Only if they make a difference are they worth the trouble. The rest of the Jamesian strategy is to reject the other constraints on truth (especially the identity of content and explanation requirements) as phantoms of an impossible abstraction of truth as a property belonging to all true claims. James's pragmatic conception of truth is still a theory of truth, but it is a reconstruction of the very project.

Russell's Criticisms

James's theory of truth has met with serious criticism from Bertrand Russell. Russell's two main criticisms of James's theory are that (a) it does not capture the meaning of truth in the requisite sense of *meaning*, and (b) it, by its own lights, is false. We will outline these criticisms in order.

'Meaning', Russell contends, is ambiguous (1966/1909: 97). On the one hand, we may say, 'That cloud of smoke *means* there is fire', and by this, we use *means* to say that one event is associated with another. We may infer that given some X, Y follows. On the other hand, we may say, 'The German word "rot" *means* what we *mean* in English by "red"'. By this we use *means* to say that a symbol in one language plays the same signifying role in another language. The project of philosophical analysis of terms is to get to the meaning of terms in the *second sense*. We want to know what the terms *signify*, what they *communicate*. This, for example, is what Socrates is up to when he asks his interlocutors what justice is. He wants to get clearer about what a term means by getting clear about what it signifies. The question of truth is not what we may expect from true beliefs, but what it is we communicate when we say a belief is true. The problem is that James's theory is one that captures the meaning of truth in only the first sense; it says that if a person has a true belief that *p*, then she will be successful with regard to her plans regarding *p*. On this analysis, James just isn't doing philosophy right.

A reasonable response for the Jamesian is that the traditional philosophical aspirations are neither feasible nor even worth talking about. They proceed from an exceedingly abstracted view of truth-talk, and James forearms his views against this challenge in formulating what he calls the *sentimentalist fallacy* of idealizing qualities of justice, beauty, and so on to the point where one may never know them when met on the street (WWJ, 440–1).

Russell seems to recognize that his first objection rests on a conception of the philosophical enterprise James rejects, and so he pursues a second line of argument in other exchanges with James. This second line is that the theory is self-referentially false. The Jamesian theory equates truth with practical success. The payoff, James promises, is that truth will be *more accessible* – we will have a highly functional way of telling true from false beliefs by how well they work out. Russell then notes:

> The notion that it is quite easy to know when the consequences of belief are good, so easy, in fact, that a theory of knowledge need take no account of anything so simple – this notion, I must say, seems to me one of the strangest assumptions for a theory of knowledge to make. (1908/1966: 119)

Pragmatism is supposed to make truth easier to grasp by tying the question of truth to the question of utility or usefulness. But it is not any easier to determine utility than it is to determine truth. Is it more or less useful to believe that the pope is infallible? Solipsism (the philosophical theory that you are the only existing thing and everything and everyone else is an illusion) is sometimes useful and sometimes not. So evaluating beliefs and theories in terms of utility, instead of making things easier, just makes things even harder. So the pragmatic theory of truth, Russell concludes, may be useless.

Further, with each of the questions posed regarding the pope and solipsism, we evaluate our beliefs with regard to their truth or falsity. We assume that beliefs are either true or false. The fact that it may, overall, be *slightly* more useful to believe the pope is infallible than not, or *sometimes* convenient to accept solipsism seems to entail that these theories are *a little true* or *a little false* depending on the outcomes. But solipsism is either true or not – you can't be the only existing thing *a little*. The pope is infallible or not – nobody, not even the pope, can be *slightly infallible*. The problem, then, is that truth and falsity are, at least on their face, *absolute terms*. Utility, however, comes in *gradients*.

One way to revise the Jamesian story is to say that some beliefs may reach a threshold of usefulness, and *that* makes them true. But this concedes that usefulness is not the whole story with truth. On this view, it's not the utility, but the threshold that matters. Further, the answer as to whether it is useful or not to believe solipsism is true seems on its face irrelevant to its truth or falsity. Surely it is more useful to believe that there are other people in the world and act accordingly, but that does not touch the question as to whether there are or are not.

It seems, again, that the Jamesian theory risks being useless. This carries us beyond Russell's criticism, but the point remains: The pragmatic theory of truth is supposed to *clarify* truth by identifying truth with usefulness; however, *usefulness* seems no less obscure a concept than truth. How *useful* are one's beliefs, really? Is that usefulness calculable and comparable to their negations? To one's abstentions? Do the smug satisfactions of those who hold some views count for the view's utility as equally as the smug satisfaction of those who reject it?

The Jamesian may respond that we cannot know the consequences of any given belief beforehand. We must experiment and live these 'truths' more as hypotheses in order to find out. James's theory, then, entails a commitment to *fallibilism:*

> Meanwhile we have to live today by what truth we can get today, and be ready tomorrow to call it falsehood. (WWJ, 438)

The objective is to find useful theories and beliefs, and though it is difficult to do so, that does not detract from the overall goods achieved by the enterprise to searching and inquiring.

James and Disagreement

There is a final point of concern we must raise with the Jamesian theory of truth, namely, that it makes no room for real disagreement between believers. What it is to hold a belief is to hold that its contents are true. If you believe that *p* is true, then you think that somebody else who holds that *p* is false is *wrong*. The problem with usefulness is that it is *relativized* to those for whom something is useful or not. For example, the belief that beef is tasty may very well be useful to someone being seated at a fine steakhouse, but it's not particularly useful for the hungry homeless outside (not to mention how badly things go for the cows). The Jamesian theory may explain *why* some people hold the beliefs they do, and it may even help us refine our beliefs in order for us to live better lives, but it is hard to make sense of how two people who disagree on a matter may see the theory as of any help. They may understand each other better, but when it comes to inquiring as to who's right, the theory seems, again, useless. This is because the utility of *p* is indexed to whomever *p* is useful for. So, someone may say, '*p* is true for me', and still say '*p* is false for you'. This of course, reduces the Jamesian theory to a form of relativism: truths are relativized to the desires and values of those who believe them.

The problem is that relativism cannot address the fact of disagreement: when two people disagree, telling them that it is all relative does not resolve their disagreement. To be sure, it may prevent them from *discussing* the matter or *giving arguments* to each other. You can't argue someone out of her tastes or desires, and if truth depends on those things, arguments are impotent. So we just have to either tolerate those with whom we disagree or find other (nonrational) ways of resolving disagreements. This is even worse. If people aren't going to discuss or argue over their differences, then there aren't too many other nonviolent ways people may settle thorny issues that divide them. One long-standing lesson of history is that we negotiate only when we can't just take what we want. The consequence is that James's theory not only prevents us from saying that someone with whom we disagree is simply wrong, but it also prevents us from engaging with anyone other than those with whom we already agree.

James's own take on the history of philosophy in the first of his *Pragmatism* lectures 'The Present Dilemma in Philosophy' reflects this attitude. James contends that there are two basic temperaments driving philosophy, the tenderminded and tough-minded. One's temperament, not one's arguments, determines one's theoretical commitments:

> The history of philosophy is to a great extent that of a certain clash of human temperaments . . . Of whatever temperament a professional philosopher is, he tries when philosophizing to sink the fact of his temperament. Temperament is no conventionally recognized reason, so he urges impersonal reasons only for his conclusions. Yet his temperament really gives him a stronger bias than any of his more strictly objective premises . . . He *trusts* his temperament. (WWJ, 363–4; italic in the original)

The consequence, then, is that *even in philosophy*, arguments do not do any good to change anyone's mind. The value of every view is something determined individually by each believer's temperament. The matter is not the truth of any of the views, but how they reflect our given inclinations – like finding shoes that fit. However, surely James holds that those who reject his view about the nature of truth and philosophical disagreement are wrong; he holds that the sentimentalist's fallacy is a *fallacy*, after all (WWJ, 440). So he must hold that traditionalists are *wrong about something*, not just of a different temperament. If not, arguing for the view further (or at all, for that matter!) would be pointless. You can't argue someone out of his temperament, remember. Since James *does* argue for the view and lay out its consequences, James himself couldn't, in the end, be committed to his own view about truth or philosophy!

PRAGMATIST EVASIONS OF TRUTH

Deweyan Replacement

In light of the difficulties confronting the very enterprise of devising a theory of truth, one might conclude that it is best simply to not have any theory of truth. We can accomplish this evasion of truth in three ways: replace truth with a more tractable concept, change the subject altogether, or positively hold truth in contempt.

Recall the Peircean theory of truth as ideal convergence. This view holds that truth is what is verified for inquirers at the end of inquiry. In his *Logic: The Theory of Inquiry*, Dewey approvingly writes of Peirce's theory as 'the best definition of truth from the logical standpoint' (LW12: 343). The problem comes with taking truth to be *equivalent* to justification for taking as true, but Dewey reasoned that there is something to the idea that we use *truth* to mean *what we have justification to believe*. Instead of defining truth in terms of those conditions that confer warrant to our beliefs, why don't we just talk about those conditions that warrant belief? For our purposes, nothing gets clarified by putting the term 'truth' in the mix. Instead, we should focus on the justification we have for holding things true. Hence Dewey:

> Truth or falsity depends on what men find when they warily perform the experiment of observing reflective events. (LW1: 35)

Further, the notion that truth is objective or subjective may be replaced by the clear fact that our experimentation and marshalling our evidence are cases of *bringing about knowledge*. This is what we were trying to capture with theories of truth to begin with, since it is something that we may control and be responsible for. This is what makes having a theory of truth worth all the effort. As a consequence, the notion of objectivity in truth is refigured, since objectivity in these conditions is not something considered as objects independent of subjects, but as something arising from the evidence:

> [I]n the practice of science, knowledge is an affair of *making* sure, not grasping antecedently given sureties. (LW1: 23; italic in the original)

On this analysis, what is worth having a theory about is the process by which knowledge and its objects arise. Truth is left as an imprecise cipher for when this knowledge is achieved. On this view, *truth* is still a success term, but one that we needn't have a theory about except in terms of what we may associate with the kind of successes we call *true belief*:

Sometimes the word 'truth' is confined to designating a logical property of propositions; but if we extend its significance to designate character of existential reference, this is the meaning of truth: processes of change so directed that they achieve an intended consummation. (LW1: 128)

Dewey was still an instrumentalist about truth, but the account was not meant to be a central element of his view, since what is important for him is the process of inquiry that brings us to know truths. However, those truths are ones we may take as true only by way of our evidence and knowledge. Hence it is better to talk of *warranted assertion* (LW12: 8–9). From the pragmatic perspective, there is no difference that makes a difference between a subject pursuing warranted beliefs and one pursuing true ones. So long as this is right, *the true* is replaceable with *the warranted*.

The primary difficulty with Dewey's view is that warranted assertion is a poor replacement for truth. Bertrand Russell, again, captures the concern best when he notes that such a replacement would be a 'cosmic impiety' (1996/1946: 737).[1] Russell holds that when we come to know, we come into contact with something outside ourselves, something not up to us. To replace or refigure such a notion with something that that is an extension of our interests is in Russell's estimation *cognitive hubris* – 'man, formerly too humble began to think of himself as almost a God' (1996/1946: 737). Such a view is not only metaphysically wrong, but is socially and intellectually disastrous.

One way to understand the intellectual disaster Russell foresees for the Deweyan program is to consider that replacing truth with warrant undermines the fallibilist core of pragmatism. A fallibilist contends that one may justifiably hold to a belief, but the belief may in the end be false. But notice that if *truth* is simply short for *justified belief*, then if someone justifiably holds a view, how does it make sense for her to say she may be wrong? Fallibilism requires that truth and justification must be different notions, that good reasons aren't necessarily guarantees of truth. But if we take truth to be short for justification, that gap dissolves.

Thus, there is a tension in Dewey's theory of cognition. If truth is warranted assertion, then it makes no sense to say our best (most warranted) scientific theories may nevertheless be false. But fallibilism requires that we acknowledge this as a real possibility.

Rorty Changes the Subject

Richard Rorty's first characterization of pragmatism in 'Pragmatism, Relativism, Irrationalism' is this:

> [I]t is simply anti-essentialism applied to notions like 'truth', 'knowledge', 'language', 'morality', and similar objects of philosophical theorizing . . . [T]ruth is not the sort of thing that has an essence. (1982: 62)

Again, the lesson of the previous sections is that most theories of truth end in shipwreck. Rorty takes it that this suggests that one cannot have a theory about these words like *truth* (and *knowledge*, *morality*, etc.) and things they purportedly name:

> Pragmatists think that the history of attempts to isolate the True . . . or to define the word 'true' . . . supports their idea that there is no interesting work to be done in this area. (1982: xiv)

Rorty holds that, instead of proposing a new method of getting at knowledge or a new definition of truth, pragmatists should just 'change the subject' (1982: xiv). The pragmatist, Rorty takes it, is in the same position as a secularist who finds that a detailed study of the wills of various gods will not help solve social or scientific problems. Rorty proposes that we should not try to *replace* those notions with more tractable ones, but change the direction of inquiry entirely. Some projects are boondoggles, and instead of debate the boondoggle (and thus prolong it), we should just stop.

Rorty's proposed new direction for inquiry is twofold: on the one hand, he proposes ironic reflection on the contingencies of our default attitudes, and on the other hand, he proposes hopeful mappings of our prospects for solidarity. We are *ironic* about the historical milieu of our discussions, the happenstances that led us to use this vocabulary instead of another to discuss a problem, and we are *hopeful* that the varieties of vocabularies and conflicts between them will not suffocate decent discussion. We must continue the conversation. We cannot escape the situation of conflict of vocabularies by redescribing it from the outside:

> For us ironists, nothing can serve as a criticism of a final vocabulary save another final vocabulary . . . Since there is nothing

beyond vocabularies which serves as a criterion of choice between them, criticism is a matter of looking on this picture or that, not of comparing both pictures with the original. (1989: 80)

Bemused compare and contrast work between cultures and languages is Rorty's research program. Philosophy, then, is reconstructed as less an exercise in wrestling with the big problems, and more a style of journalistic or autobiographical composition:

> Philosophy is best seen as a kind of writing. It is delimited, as any literary genre, not by a form or matter, but by tradition – a family romance involving, e.g., Father Parmenides, Uncle Kant, and bad brother Derrida. (1982: 92)

Of course, *truth* is a term that functions centrally to some of those traditions in philosophical writing, but Rorty holds that this literary movement has played out – think of how words like 'alas' or 'thou' sound silly coming from our mouths, but just fine out of a poet in Elizabethan England. We simply no longer talk that way; those words don't have any more use in our lives. According to Rorty, *truth* in those fancy philosophical usages is in the same boat as the Elizabethan poet's *thou*.

The problem for Rorty's view is that truth just doesn't go away that easily. Rorty's metaphilosophical view about philosophy as a kind of writing conflicts with his views about truth precisely for this reason. Rorty notes that there is plenty of resistance to his view that philosophy is simply a style of writing. The tradition, in essence, 'does not think that philosophy *should* be "written" any more than science should be. Writing is an unfortunate necessity' (1982: 94). That is, the opposing view is that philosophy is wrestling with the big ideas, and the writing is what comes later, the tale of the outcome of the wrestling. But Rorty thinks that those who oppose him are *wrong*; he holds that they have a *false* view of the nature of philosophy. If philosophy is a style of writing, then these traditionalists don't just have another style of writing, they are *wrong* about what they are doing. If this is right, then for traditionalists to be wrong to reject the philosophy as a style of writing thesis, the thesis must be true in more than just the way some style just uses the word *true*. It has to be true in the way the opposition uses the term. But if the view that philosophy is just a style of writing is true in this way, then the nature of truth does matter: Rorty indeed *criticizes* those who reject the view, right?

As a consequence, truth resurfaces even in Rorty's evasive program, since for the program to make sense at all, it must be taken as a *corrective* of traditional philosophy. But this renders it self-defeating.

Stich's Rejection

We have seen that developing a coherent view on truth is tough business. We have presumed thus far that the task is worthwhile, since truth is something worthwhile. But perhaps it isn't. Stephen Stich has forwarded two arguments that truth is not worth caring about.

Stich's first argument is that our beliefs are true or false depending both on what we believe and how the world is. How things are in the world is difficult enough to determine, but what we believe is also open to interpretation. Stich hews to a stark naturalism (to be discussed in our chapter on metaphysics), and Stich's take on the mind entails that beliefs are brain states that represent things in the world. For them to be *about* those things, they must be interpreted to be representations. In order for written sentences (arrangements of marks on paper), pictures (arrangements of pigment on canvas), or maps (arrangements of lines and figures) to be *about* their objects, there needs to be interpretive schemes that connect them up. So with beliefs, too, we need interpretations in order to make them represent. But there are a variety of interpretive schemes for them to have the functional features they do.

We will address the functional elements of belief on interpretations in the next chapter; however, it is clear from what we have here, that on one interpretation, a belief can come out true, while on another, it is false. For example, many beliefs' truth or falsity depends on how one's terms are defined. The gold watch Sam bought for $15 on the street is *gold* in the sense that it is *colored gold*, but it is not *gold* in the sense that the atoms making it up have an atomic number of 79. We can keep track of the truth or falsity of these interpretations by starring 'truth' when we attribute it to the belief under one interpretation or another. On the first interpretation, then, the belief is *true*, but on the second, the belief is *false**. The point here is that we are talking about the same belief and the same facts in the world, but now we can't explain why truth is really preferable to falsity. Any time we have a false belief, a bit of reinterpreting the terms will make it *true* or true***, but it won't change the belief or the world. How is that valuable?

There are two problems for Stich's first argument. The first is simply that Stich has presumed that truth is broadly like the correspondence theory we charted earlier: interpretation here plays the role of explaining how a belief can correspond to the world. If that's that case, then Stich's argument provides not a demonstration that *truth* is not valuable, but that *truth as a kind of correspondence* is not valuable.[2]

The second problem is that Stich's argument is based on the presumption that beliefs, in order to represent, must be *interpreted*, and further, that the variety of interpretations are not determined or limited by the belief. But this doesn't seem right from the perspective of believers. When we believe, we do so on an interpretation of what the facts are. If the meanings of the terms or the interpretation change, then our beliefs would change. Return to the watch case above. Now that we are aware of the two interpretations, we no longer see the belief that Sam has a gold watch as a singular belief, but as a *statement of belief* that is ambiguous between Sam having a *gold-colored* watch and Sam having a watch *made of gold*. We will return to this problem in the metaphysics chapter.

This brings us to Stich's second argument, one that flies directly against the classical pragmatist view that truth is instrumentally valuable. Stich argues truth is sometimes the last thing we need. Say that Harry believes truly that his plane will take off at 7:45 p.m. He arrives early, gets a good seat, and gets ready for take off. The plane then crashes, and Harry dies a fiery death. Wouldn't a false belief about what time take off was have been better – preferably one that would have gotten him to the airport well after the crash? Harry would have missed his flight (too bad), but he would not have died (whew!). So here, it seems, truth is sometimes bad for you. The consequence is that truth isn't (or shouldn't be) what we are out to pursue with reasoning and believing. Stich offers the following replacement:

> Cognitive processes, pragmatists will insist, should not be thought of primarily as devices for generating truths. Rather they should be thought of as something akin to tools or technologies or practices that can be used more or less successfully in achieving a variety of goals. (1993: 131)

The first problem with this argument is that Stich picks out the wrong belief for Harry. The one that truly matters is Harry's presumption that the plane will fly safely. There are plenty of other beliefs that would keep him off the plane (e.g., the false belief that the fastest way to the airport would be to ride a turtle). But because the airplane crashes, the belief that matters is the one bearing on the safety of the flight. If Harry believed truly that flying on that plane was dangerous, those other beliefs (true or false) wouldn't matter. So it is not an issue about the number of true or false beliefs that bears on the instrumental value of truth, but on the relevance of the belief at issue.[3]

The second problem with Stich's view is that it is self-defeating. Stich steps squarely on the intellectual banana peel when he says:

> True beliefs are not always optimal in the pursuit of happiness or pleasure or desire satisfaction, nor are they always the best beliefs to have if we want peace or power or love or some weighted mix of these. (1993: 123)

But surely he takes it that it is *better* to have an accurate picture of the situation with truth.

PRAGMATISM AND DEFLATIONISM

The Appeal of Deflation

Recall that Frege's regress argument was posed as a problem for any theory of truth. And so it seems we cannot have any substantive theory of truth. However, we have seen that the aspiration of evading a theory truth is equally hopeless – to not care for truth and its nature is at best deluded and at worst self-defeating. So it seems we are caught between two inconsistent requirements.

Deflationism is an attempt to squeeze between the two obstacles. The aim is to say enough about truth to avoid the self-defeat of evasion, but not say so much so as to run headlong into the Frege regress. One way to put the deflationist's thesis is to say that the prerequisite that we'd called the Equivalence Requirement (*p* is true iff *p*) is all there is to say about truth. Frege himself anticipated this outcome when he posed his regress, in that he remarked:

> 'I smell the scent of violets' has just the same content as 'It is true that I smell the scent of violets'. So it seems, then, that nothing

is added to the thought by ascribing to it the property of truth. (1997: 328)

When we say that it is true that Frege smells violets, it may appear that we are talking about a thought, sentence, or proposition and it having a certain property of truth. But we are really talking about Frege and what he smells. Thus, Frank Ramsey notes, when we add 'is true' to any claim, we do not add anything to it at all (1964/1927: 16–17). To say of a claim that it is true is simply gratuitous or redundant; we are saying exactly the same thing we would have said just by making the claim.

Thus, the term *truth* still plays a role in our language, but it is a restricted role, namely, that of *disquotation*. When someone says of any sentence that it is true, she must put the sentence in quotation marks. So someone may say of a sentence (s) that it is true, so she would have to say:

's' is true.

So let the sentence 'The cat is on the mat' be true, and so our subject says:

'The cat on the mat' is true.

When we hear our subject utter that sentence, we should just take her to simply be asserting that the cat is on the mat. So we interpret her sentence as directing us to take the quotation marks off the sentence and ignore the 'is true' words, and just pay attention to the sentence as an assertion (Quine 1970).

The benefit of the deflationary take on truth is that it is utterly minimalist: there is no substantial view of the term *truth* beyond its logical and linguistic functions. We do not have to view it as a property of beliefs, sentences or propositions, and there is nothing that need prevent us from doing so, either. It is only that this is all there is to be said about truth that *must* be said. So the deflationary move appeals to many contemporary pragmatists, since it avoids the excesses of the old substantial versions of truth without tripping up on the problems with evasion.

Another benefit of the deflationary take on truth is that it represents the tight connection between the use of the term *true* with claims and that of making the claims. Using the term *true* is a form of making an assertion. The combination of these two benefits of deflationism produces a paradigmatically pragmatist outlook: that we have a theory that avoids pointless metaphysics about a term and turns our attention to the practices of its use.

Deflationism and Normativity

The deflationist program is posited on the thought that in light of the Frege regress, the less one says about the nature of truth beyond the identity requirement, the better. The problem is that this may not be enough. Let us start with truth and normativity: *truth* is a success term. If the term *true* is redundant in its usage, then it seems silly, awkward, and counterproductive for having such a term in a language. If saying a claim is true is just a long-winded way of asserting the claim, *true* is a useless term, one that wastes our time and risks wasting further time with metaphysics. Deflationism is a short step from eliminativism.

Further, deflationary views of *truth* as simply a *term* seems to put *the way we talk about truth* in the place of *truth itself.* That is, deflationism treats truth like it is just a word, and as a consequence, it undercuts any way we could articulate its value. Take by analogy, a move to replace the question about the value of art with the question about the value of *the term art.* The *value* of true beliefs gets, well . . . deflated. And once it is deflated in this way, it is not clear why we want truth to begin with beyond the fact that we treat beliefs we call true better than ones we call false. True sentences play an important role in our languages, for example, as premises in arguments. But surely it must be the other way around: we value the validity of an inference because truth-preservation (and truth) is valuable, not the other way around.

Deflationists can answer the normativity challenge, to a degree. First, the question as to why we have the term *truth* at all may be answered by noting that terms like *true, false,* and other logical-semantic vocabulary allow us a *metalanguage* that gives us the terms to talk about how we and others reason and take things to stand in the world. Truth (and the other logical-semantic terms) allow us a set of tools to analyze our concepts and reasonings critically. This is what Quine calls 'semantic ascent':

It is the shift from talk about miles to talk of 'mile'. It is what leads from the material . . . mode into the formal mode, to invoke an old terminology of Carnap's. It is the shift from talking in certain terms to talking about them. (1960: 271)

The truth term is part of a language making semantic ascent possible, so that is why it is valuable. However, this answer runs directly into the teeth of the second normativity worry: it treats truth as simply a term. Once we switch over to the formal mode with semantic terms, we can't go back. As a consequence, truth as what is said of beliefs, propositions, and sentences is left out of the story; all we have is *truth* as a term functioning in a language of commentary. This is too thin. This cannot be the *meaty* value of truth.

One way to address this secondary worry is to supplement deflationism with the view that beliefs aim at truth – it is a *norm of beliefs* that makes truth valuable. So a theory of truth just must not run afoul of this norm of beliefs, instead of explaining the value of truth all by itself. We will explore this connection next.

Deflationism and Explanation

Recall that the explanation prerequisite for theories of truth says that the truth or falsity of a claim is explained by what the claim is about. If you say that *Bill Clinton is a Martian*, that's false because he isn't. If you say *Bill Clinton is from Arkansas*, that's true, because he is. The way the world is determines whether or not our beliefs are true, and we inquire so as to find out how the world is. Deflationists have no way of accommodating this thought beyond interpreting the term *because* in the explanations to be the identity of meaning between the two sentences. But that's not the kind of explanation needed because identity relations are symmetric: it doesn't matter which side of the relation either is on. But if the world explains why our beliefs are true, it doesn't follow that our belief's truth explains why the world is the way it is. With the normativity problem earlier, deflationism replaces properties with terms in semantic ascent. Now, with the explanation problem, deflationism replaces metaphysical relations of explanation with logical relations of equivalence. These are unsatisfying replacements.

One defense is to say that deflationism is supposed to be metaphysically neutral. Shouldering such a burden of explanation is beyond

PRAGMATISM: A GUIDE FOR THE PERPLEXED

the scope of the theory, and not addressing it is, instead of a *vice*, is one of its *central virtues*. Instead of viewing the explanation scheme as a prerequisite for a theory of truth, we should view it as a holdover from the times when the correspondence theory was in vogue. With the failure of that theory, we should forego the requirements that made it so appealing, too.

However, a complete break with the requirement is not entirely necessary. Cheryl Misak and Christopher Hookway treat the pragmatist take on truth as bearing a strong resemblance to deflationism, but the pragmatist approporation is not the exceedingly thin theory we may take deflationism to be. If we, again, note that saying a claim is true is equivalent to asserting it, we note that first, we lend our *assent* to the claim, and moreover, we assert according to the rule of assertion that we have evidence for what we claim. Hookway reasons:

> Describing something as true involves taking up a 'normative stance or attitude towards' it: it is to endorse it and to incur various normatively grounded commitments to it. For example: we commit ourselves to the expectation that future experiment and experience will not require us to withdraw our claim. (2002: 64)

The consequence here is that the explanatory element of truth is no longer metaphysical, but epistemic; we hold the claim true because it fits our evidence, and we expect it to continue to do so. We may remain metaphysically neutral regarding the objects of inquiry, since there are times when it seems right to take objects as independent entities (e.g., the contents of stars or the laws of physics) and others as dependent on our interests (e.g., truths about politics). Misak similarly notes that a Peircean notion of continued inquiry elucidates truth in a neutral fashion: 'A belief is true if it would fully satisfy the requirements and standards of inquiry' (2007: 88). The questions of metaphysics will arise (if they must) within the specific inquiries, and so a theory of truth need not address these issues. Instead, the only explanation one needs on the level of truth is why one would say that the claim is true, and the answer is that because it is supported by the evidence.

The upshot is that a Peircean-inspired form of deflationism can make up some ground against the normativity and explanation problems. However, a final worry hangs for those Peircean deflationists.

Have they replaced a theory of truth with a theory of inquiry? Truth is a stand-in here, again like on Peirce's convergence model, for a belief surviving critical scrutiny from all possible quarters. This is no longer a theory of truth, but rather a 'pragmatic elucidation' of the notion (Misak 2004a: vii). So it seems inappropriate to hold it to the test of the Frege regress. However, it seems a kind of bait and switch has occurred here. Is the deflationary pragmatist theory of truth simply an epistemology or optimistic theory of inquiry in disguise?

CHAPTER 4

PRAGMATISM AND METAPHYSICS

METAPHYSICS AND ULTIMATE REALITY

Preliminaries

In the previous chapters, we have referred to subjects and their beliefs, objects and their properties, the world, and reality, without offering much of an explanation of them. But what is the world? What is a subject, and what is it for one to have a belief? What makes something real? These are questions of *metaphysics*.

Metaphysics is best described as the study of ultimate reality. In ordinary language, we have a basic grasp of this notion of ultimate reality in that we understand the contrast between appearance and reality: appearances are only what seem to be, and reality is what really is. A theory of knowledge tells us how to get at what really is, and a theory of truth tells us what it is to be right about what is real. Metaphysics, however, is the study of what is real, full stop. Classically, metaphysics has been divided between two kinds of questions. The first kind is that of *general metaphysics*, or *ontology*: what things exist, and what it is for things to exist. The second kind concerns the nature of things that are, and these are the issues of *special metaphysics*: whether there is a God, whether humans have free will, what it is to have an identity, the relation between the mind and the body, and so on.

Prior to the modern period of philosophy, metaphysics was generally done from what might be called a *theological* perspective, from God's view of things. Given what take one has on God and His relationship to the rest of reality, one fashions one's metaphysics accordingly. This was a tidy philosophical strategy until doubts about our reasons for taking God to be one way or another (or to exist at all) came to the front. Unless we have a means to determine which theology is right, we don't have a means to proceed with any story of reality. This led many of the modern philosophers to press the questions of epistemology first. With the modern project of developing accounts of knowledge, the standard strategy was to turn metaphysics out of these successful takes on knowledge. The success of the natural sciences in developing detailed and reliable knowledge about how things work yielded a scientific program in metaphysics called *naturalism*. The early pragmatists were enthusiastic naturalists, and their attitudes within metaphysics were generally consequences of this organizing view.

In this chapter, we will follow the classical division between general and special metaphysics. We will first lay out the ontology that is entailed by pragmatist naturalism. We will then turn to critically survey specific applications of pragmatist naturalism with the question of God's nature and existence, the relations between body and mind, and what it is for something to be an individual thing.

NATURALISM AND PRAGMATISM

An Anatomy of Naturalism

Naturalism is a two-part view. The first part is a methodological commitment as to how inquiry should proceed; it contends that philosophy generally, and metaphysics specifically, should be conducted within the framework provided by our best scientific theories of how the basic elements of nature are constituted and interact. Naturalists hold that there is a *continuity*, not only of the *standards* for successful research between philosophy and the sciences, but also of the *findings* of the respective areas. Thus, just as scientific theories may be overturned by new evidence or rebutted by others working in the field, so may philosophical theories.[1] We can recognize the core of this commitment in the fallibilist component of pragmatist epistemology. What is new here is that the fallibilist outlook modeled on the sciences integrates the notions of *empirical evidence, experiment,* and *public scrutiny* of one's findings to yield a broad conception of inquiry. Further, we can see the ways in which this methodological commitment is related to pragmatist takes on truth. Peirce argued for methodological naturalism on the basis of the scientific method's virtues of fixing belief in a fallibilist and public-experimental procedure:

> I may start with known and observed facts to proceed to the unknown; and yet the rules which I follow in doing so may not be such as investigation would approve. The test of whether I am truly following the method is not an immediate appeal to my feelings and purposes, but, on the contrary, itself involves application of the method. (CP, 5.385)

The scientific method is self-correcting. Given our openness to counterevidence with public scrutiny of our reasonings, the method in being applied, will root out its other misapplications.

The second part of naturalism is an ontological view – a view about the nature of the real. It can be summarized as follows: All that is, including every property of what is, is natural. These natural things and their properties conform to regular laws, they may be studied by the methods of science relevant to those laws, and they all exist in a world where they share some measure of (potential) causal interaction. Peirce states his ontology as one of a scientific metaphysics posited on what we had named in Chapter 1 'The Hypothesis of Reality':

> [Science's] fundamental hypothesis . . . is this: There are Real things, whose characters are entirely independent of our opinions about them; those Reals affect our senses according to regular laws, and . . . by taking advantage of the laws of perception, we can ascertain by reasoning how things really and truly are. (CP, 5.384)

With this hypothesis, we see the two components of naturalism are mutually implicated: all things that are real are things that can be studied according to the methods of science.

Pragmatic naturalism, however, involves a third component. Pragmatism is a form of *Humanism*, one which requires that philosophical and scientific work be extensions of and relevant to the values and purposes of human lives. The objects of concern for our theoretical enterprises are those of improving our lives, of safeguarding what is valuable, and of opening new possibilities. Philosophical reflection that spurns the human significance of its findings is worthless theorizing. William James captures this requirement well:

The whole function of philosophy ought to be to find out what difference it would make to you and me, at definite instants of our life, if this world-formula or that world-formula be the true one. (WWJ, 379)

To engage in the pursuit of the real independently of the consequences for human life is to take on what Dewey calls 'the spectator theory of knowledge', one that fails to account for the situational context of inquiry (LW4: 163). Philosophical and scientific questions arise from problems in the situated researches of inquirers. Knowledge arises as a natural phenomenon, then, one that involves not just the world and a knower, but the interaction between the two. Humans are biological entities in complicated environments, each with its constitution. Human thought and its objects should be described as the outgrowth of the interaction of such an organism with its environs.

Consequences of Pragmatist Naturalism

There are two consequences of this broad program of pragmatist naturalism. First is that pragmatists take on the project of *nonreductive metaphysics*. Nonpragmatist naturalist programs attempt to reduce the social, valuational, and aesthetic elements of human life to the biology or chemistry of the human animal; on these views, there might not be much more to virtue than instinct, or to beauty than evolution's hardwiring in our brains. The humanistic element of pragmatism rejects reductionism, requiring that we view the questions that animate human life on their own terms.

Pragmatic metaphysics, then, in pursuing the real, also strives to save the appearances. For many of these appearances to be saved, however, they must be *reconstructed*. This brings us to the second consequence of pragmatist naturalism: issues of great import to humans that seem to be not investigable scientifically are reformulated so that they may be. Call this *reconstructive metaphysics*. Peirce's positivism was a stark requirement of reconstruction: one's whole conception of a thing is what practical effects could be inferred from its existence (CP, 5.402). Peirce's application of the criterion yielded not only clarifications of certain properties of things (e.g., hardness, weight, and force) but also the revelation that some inquiries were not worth pursuing or were posited on nonsense. Remember from Chapter 1 the issue of *transubstantiation* – the question of whether the wine and wafer of Catholic Eucharist are, despite appearances, *really* the blood and body of Christ. Peirce proposes that the theological debate either be reframed so that empirical evidence may provide traction for a good answer or it should be dropped altogether. Alternately, James's account of the Eucharist in terms of the consequences of *believing in it* is such a reconstruction.

Three Problems

Before turning to pragmatist special metaphysics, let us sketch some problems with pragmatist naturalism. The first problem for pragmatist metaphysics is integrating humanism with naturalism. The human perspective is clearly a function of our evolutionary heritage – we are hominids with brains and perceptual organs that were selected for in an environment where hunting, gathering, and avoiding getting eaten by big animals were important. Those systems may function the way they do, not because they are *right* about our environment, but because they simply helped us *survive*. From the perspective of physics, a good number of our commonsense properties risk not being real about things at all (e.g., color, solidity, impenetrability), and so from a naturalist's view of things, humanism and its requirements of nonreduction or elimination blocks the road of inquiry. Thus Quine,

> Physics investigates the essential nature of the world, and biology describes a local bump. Psychology, human psychology, describes a bump on a bump. (1981: 93)

Similarly, Wilfrid Sellars distinguishes the *manifest image* (how we take things as we get around in the world) and the *scientific image* (how things are from the perspective of our best scientific theories). He then notes that his 'critique of the manifest image . . . compares this image unfavorably with a *more* intelligible account of what there is', namely, the scientific image (2007/1962: 397; italic in the original). It seems that naturalism and humanism, though allies in urging that research should be relevant and helpful to human life, are on the road to being rivals.

The second problem for naturalism generally is that of explaining the norms of scientific inquiry as being truth-directed even though they arose merely from animals trying to survive. That is, if most of the mechanisms of human cognition were formed by evolutionary pressures of the Pleistocene savannas of Africa, then scientific method is a formalized expression of the coping mechanisms of hunter-gatherer hominids. That is, if we see the results of human inquiry on the model of an organism trying to maintain a stable relationship with its environment, why should we take any of that organism's resultant commitments to be *true*, as opposed to *merely convenient?* G. E. Moore famously argued that to understand normative questions (e.g., those of the rules of reasoning and living well, what is good, true, and beautiful) from the perspective of naturalism or any descriptive empirical inquiry, is to commit *the naturalistic fallacy* (1903: 59). And so if *good* or *true* means what brings an organism into a stable relationship with its environment, then it would be self-contradictory to say that something brings stability but is not true or good. But not only is it *not* a contradiction to say such a thing, it is often correct. Think of noble lies in politics, fibs to get along with others better, and other useful dissemblance. We will address this problem more fully in the next chapter on ethics as the *is/ought* problem.

Third and finally, there is the question of demarcation for the sciences that yield legitimate and relevant answers for our philosophical research. It seems that some sciences are taken as paradigmatic, specifically physics and chemistry, and others have their place depending on how they live up to the standards set by the paradigm sciences. But the question hangs: what distinguishes these nonparadigmatic sciences that are nonetheless legitimate (e.g., biology) from the ones that are nonparadigmatic and not legitimate (e.g., parapsychology)? A regular answer to what Karl Popper called 'the demarcation problem' of distinguishing science from pseudoscience is that the methods and theories of the sciences are *testable* or *falsifiable* (1962: 39). That is, a theory is legitimate if there could be an experiment devised so that if the theory is right, some consequences can be expected. If different consequences come about, we may infer that the theory is false.

The problem, however, is that the criterion for falsifiability is exceedingly stringent. Not all sciences we take as legitimate live up to this criterion (it has been reasonably claimed that some elements of evolutionary biology and cosmology have difficulty here), but we nevertheless hold these to be legitimate sciences. Moreover, there are questions as to what exactly it takes to falsify a theory to begin with: every time an experiment does not turn out in accord with the theory, one can always say that one thing about the circumstances weren't right.[2] The consequence of this third problem, of course, is not that pragmatist naturalism is false, but that it is less simple than it is often made out to be.

PRAGMATISM AND GOD

Dewey's Common Faith

The natural sciences have been overwhelming successes in yielding knowledge about the world. One upshot of the successes of the sciences is that theology plays a progressively smaller and smaller role in the explanations for how things work. The natural world is self-contained, and explanations come from within. There seems to be no room for God traditionally conceived, and, besides, there's nothing for Him to do. It is a truism that once one adopts a naturalistic attitude, the gods recede to obscurity and then oblivion. The pragmatists, however, still ventured to bring God back by taking on the project of *reconstructive theology*.

Dewey distinguished between *religion* and the *religious* so as to capture what is left when the gods recede. Religion is the set of dogmas and practices posited on a commitment to supernatural entities and their interest and intervention in the world. In contrast, the religious is that part of experience that, when separated from supernatural beings that grow up around it, is a natural expression of wonder at and appreciation for the world. So Dewey proposes a 'Common Faith', one where God is reconstructed:

> Suppose for the moment that the word 'God' means the ideal ends that at any given time and place one acknowledge as having authority over his volition and emotion, the values to which one is supremely devoted, so far as these ends, through imagination, take on unity. (LW9: 42)

God, then, instead of being an entity outside of and grounding our world, is reformulated as a center of social gravity. God is what holds our basic social institutions together – a natural hope that the goods we care about are worth the trouble. With the notion of the religious, Dewey hopes to preserve religion's motivational power and aspirational elements without any commitment to supernaturalist dogma. This, Dewey, takes it, is what the core of religious life is. Theology and supernatural dogma arose when we felt that hope was not enough, so we needed what we supposed was a guarantee from a protector god or the commands of a law-giver and punisher god to hold changes at bay (LW9: 78).

One question regarding Dewey's account is how well this reconstruction passes the test of those who still believe. Can one claim to be religious in this manner but have no supernatural commitments? In a sense, if you can be a thoroughgoing naturalist and be committed to social goods and peace for humans, then calling that attitude *religious* stretches the term so thinly that it is hardly recognizable any more. This may be the point of reconstruction, but many who take it that terms like *religiosity* and *religiousness* have the pull they do because of their supernaturalist or mystical elements will certainly wince at the thought that naturalist humanism also counts as being religious. Further, many naturalists will equally blanch at the term *religious*, since if it simply means *wonder* or *community*, or *love,* then we should just use those terms and avoid all the confusion. We will return to this issue at the end of this section.[3]

James's Will to Believe

James held a similarly reconstructed conception of God. The belief in God, for James, is entirely a practical affair, and it is an attitude that James took to be one that orients one's life with regard to the goods one pursues. Additionally, James reasoned that every person faces the religious hypothesis and must choose to assent to the hypothesis or reject it – to abstain from judging with regard to it is tantamount to rejecting it. The choice between theism and nontheism, is what James calls a *genuine* option. It is *live* (in that one sees oneself in the decision), it is *forced* (in that one may not opt out of the decision), and it is *momentous* (in that it is important). Religious attitudes amount, on James's reconstruction, to differing attitudes toward the universe. How one carries oneself in life is very much a function as to how one sees the world.

Further, James held that under the conditions of a genuine option being forced upon a person, that person may follow his temperament instead of his evidence. He may employ a kind of *will to believe.* This is not an endorsement of wishful thinking, but instead recognition that in holding that there are eternal things and that one is better for holding them, *one actually brings these facts about.* Take, for example, making friends. The more confident we are that we can make friends with others, the more likely that we will be successful at making friends (WWJ, 730). James holds that there is a power to thinking positively, and the commitment to reconstructed theism is a form of such a situation:

There are cases where a fact cannot come at all unless a preliminary faith exists in its coming. And where faith in a fact can help create the fact, that would be an insane logic would say that faith running ahead of scientific evidence is the lowest kind of immorality into which a thinking being can fall. (WWJ, 731)

The requirements of naturalism are to follow the evidence of the sciences and proportion one's belief to what that evidence supports. This view is sometimes termed *evidentialism*. The crucial part of James's argument is that evidentialism is wrong with regard to beliefs in something like the religious hypothesis, since believing in it brings it about.

Evidentialism, however, is not so easily refuted, since if there is evidence that there are cases where the power of positive thinking is appropriate, then one is within one's evidential rights to believe accordingly. Now the burden is on James to show that believing in eternal things will bring about their eternality and their worthiness of living one's life for them. This is an empirical hypothesis. So the empiricist-evidentialist will ask: where is James's data? In defense, the proof is in the pudding, James might claim. Life is a risk. But the question is then Why not take the risk with naturalism and use the methods and means provided by the sciences to preserve the things that are valued. We don't really need *eternal* goods, anyway; goods durable enough for a human lifetime are good enough. Pursuing only the eternal seems, well, *unpragmatic.*

West's Prophetic Pragmatism

Cornel West similarly reconstructs the language of religion within a naturalist framework he calls *prophetic pragmatism*. West's reconstruction pursues two goals: one of resolving the metaphysical tension between traditional theology and pragmatist naturalism, and the other of providing a liberatory story for religious believers. The metaphysical point is simply that one should reinterpret theological language as a commentary on culture, and see religious disagreements as attempts to transform or solidify traditions (1986: 54; 1989: 230). As a consequence, West keeps his religious commitments for what he calls 'existential' reasons – holding to the tradition is 'indispensable for me to remain sane' (1989: 233). That is, religious language is the medium through which many may capture the values that animate their lives; without religious commitments, West holds, many will be bereft of a way of discussing what is most important to them. The political point, then, is that religious language is *useful*. It not only captures unique ways in which the goods many care about are understood, but it is also a medium by which cultural change can be motivated:

> The prophetic religious person . . . puts a premium on educating and being educated by struggling peoples . . . This political dimension of prophetic pragmatism as practiced within the Christian tradition compels one to be an organic intellectual . . . Of course, he or she need be neither religious nor linked to religious institutions. (1989: 234)

That is, it is important for progressively-minded pragmatists, if they want to change society, to speak the language of those whom they want to help. As West notes, 'the culture of the wretched of the earth is deeply religious' (1989: 233). Religious language is indispensable in such grassroots work, since to forego it is to forego the way in which people state their aspirations and talk about their values.

A difficulty looms for West's reconstructive program, however, since the political element seems to endorse paternalistic attitudes toward those the pragmatist is out to help. The thought is that the prophetic pragmatist, even if she is not a religious believer, must use the language of religious belief in order to convince those she wants to help to do what she knows is best. Reconstruction is work *for the prophets*, but in order for it to be effective, the people in the church mustn't know that the prophet is reconstructing their religion. In fact, it is important that the members of the community not only not know that the prophetic pragmatist is a reconstructionist, but they themselves can't be reconstructionists themselves. As Caleb Clanton has noted regarding West's prophetic pragmatism:

> [W]hen the pragmatist maintains religious fellowship with the traditional religious believers for political purposes, the pragmatist

not only sees the religious belief of the traditional believers around him to be conceived in an intellectually immature manner, but he also banks on their maintaining their immature belief structure in order to most efficiently pursue and achieve his political purposes. (2008: 52)

That is, the success of prophetic pragmatism depends on what is taken as the ignorance of others. Religious language, then, is useful for the prophetic pragmatist because it is a powerful manipulative tool. West treats this as a reason to *promote* this language, but the consequences of the language yielding a more malleable populace is, from the perspective of democratic ideals (and ones that West is clearly also committed to), a reason *against* it. We will pursue the political issues further in Chapter 6.

The General Problem for Reconstructive Theology

A broader difficulty for reconstructive theology is this: once we have reconstructed religious commitments and language into terms comfortable to the naturalist, there will be no reason to use religious language any more. Dewey anticipated this problem in proposing his Common Faith:

> The view will seem . . . to cut the vital nerve of the religious element itself in taking away the basis upon which traditional religions and institutions have been founded. (LW9: 4)

If the importance of religious language and practice is articulable in naturalist terms, why bother with religious language and practice at all? It leads all too often to metaphysical confusion and it is even more open to abuse. Even from naturalists. Instead, why not use a clearer-headed and unquestionably naturalist language? Further, once we see the language and practices of religion under the auspices of naturalism, we would merely play act our devotionals and ape the rituals. Is prayer really *prayer* for naturalists? Further, if what we mean by 'God' is hope or love, then let us use 'hope' or 'love', and leave God alone. If God exists, He needs no reconstruction, and if he does not exist, then *we* need no reconstruction of Him.

PRAGMATISM AND THE MIND

Pragmatism and Functionalism

What is it to have a belief? In Chapter 2, we argued that to believe something is to hold some thought, proposition, or sentence true. But how does an animal with a skull full of gray goop do that? First, it clearly has to do with what is going on in the goop – the brain must be in some material state. However, this isn't enough, since it seems two very different people, or perhaps two entities with very different brains (perhaps one is a Martian), can *both* believe that the cat is on the mat. These brains aren't all in the same state, but they can have the same belief. How could that be?

One idea is that we say these beings have this belief because they *act accordingly* – they respond appropriately when asked about the mat, they are careful not to step on the cat when they wipe their feet on the mat, and so on. This is to say that the brain states these folks have must, for them to count as beliefs, play a *functional* role in their overall behavior; what makes a brain state a belief is how it contributes to the process of responding to stimuli. Mental states, then, are states that are *functional*. These functions are broadly causal or conditional relations between stimuli and other mental states on the one hand and external behavior on the other hand. So beliefs are beliefs and have the content they do because they are formed as a consequence of and are functionally related to our responses to the world impinging on us. This general take on the mind is termed *functionalism*.

Peirce's functionalism with regard to belief is that beliefs are habits of action. Beliefs are dispositions to behave a certain way under the right conditions:

> Our beliefs guide and shape our actions . . . The feeling of believing is more or less a sure indication of there being established in our nature some habit which will determine our action. (CP, 5.371)

The functional unit for James, similarly, is that of the *habit* – the proclivities an agent has under prescribed conditions. James takes belief to be a functional antecedent of action, and he reasons that the differences in the content of beliefs are to be articulated in the differences of the actions they lead to:

> If there were any part of a thought that made not difference in the thought's practical consequences, then that part would be no proper element of the thought's significance. (WWJ, 348)

James further argued that this take on the mind bears not only on beliefs, but also on consciousness. In 'Does Consciousness Exist?' James argues that the subjective elements of representing are characterized by how they yield objectively distinct actions.

Hilary Putnam's *machine–state functionalism* (1960) is based on an analogy between the mind and a machine capable of computing some input through a set of algorithms and turning out a set of outputs. The machines are called *Turing Machines*, after the mathematician Alan Turing, and the design plan for the machines is that the states of the machine at each point of input is defined in terms of its causal role in the whole system of inputs and outputs for the machine. So the machine states not only activate actions depending on what the inputs are, but also in terms of what the other machine states are. This is supposed to map beliefs' functional role, in that beliefs yield actions when appropriately connected to a number of other beliefs and desires. For example, your belief that some object is a chocolate chip cookie will yield the action of you eating it, on the conditions that you actually want a cookie and you don't believe it is poisoned. Putnam proposes that two systems (minds and machines) can be in the same kind of mental states if they bear some measure of functional isomorphism to each other:

> Two systems are functionally isomorphic if there is a correspondence between the states of one and the states of the other that preserves functional relations. (1996/1974: 133–4)

Consequently, the functionalist brings us to a position where not only empirical and manipulable models for cognition may be proposed, but where they also may be built and experimented with.

Functionalism, then, is a natural outgrowth of pragmatic naturalism. Functionalist pragmatism in its early stages was posited on the role beliefs played in practical action, but later pragmatists took the functionalist line in the direction of linguistic behavior. Sellars's model for beliefs and their content was that of how a subject uses a language to talk about what she holds to be true. On Sellars's view, speaking a language is precisely identical to the capacity to manipulate the concepts that comprise belief:

[A] proper understanding of the nature and status of linguistic rules is a *sine qua non* of a correct interpretation of the sense in which linguistic behavior can be said to *be* (and not merely express) conceptual activity. (2007/1969: 57)

As a consequence, we should view not only the beliefs of subjects from a functional perspective, but also what they mean when they speak in a functional framework:

To say what a person says, or more generally, to say *what* a kind of utterance says, is to give a functional classification of the utterance. (2007/1974: 85; italic in the original)

Thinking that *p* is to have a short-term propensity to say that *p* under the right circumstances, and what one means by '*p*' is articulable in terms of the functional role that '*p*' plays in the spoken language used by the subject. We learn the rules for responding to stimuli, and those stimuli are things we can think about like real concept-using and reasoning thinkers only after we have acquired the language of responding to them. What comes out of this linguistic-functionalist model for beliefs, thoughts, and their contents is what Sellars calls 'verbal behaviorism' (2007/1974: 83).

This prompts a regular response to the functionalist program, and especially to the extremes to which it may be taken. The mind can't be *just that*. A theory of mind that leaves out what it's like to see red *from the inside* or the felt force of one's convictions when one *really believes* must be missing something important about the mind. What it is to have an experience, have a belief, feel a desire, surely may be studied from the outside as having functional and causal features, but there is something ineliminably interior about these sorts of states. One way to get at this thought is to imagine a world where people acted the same way we do, but they don't have interior experiences. They may respond to red things appropriately, but there are not impingements of redness in their consciousness. They may say things with confidence, but they do not *feel* the confidence in their beliefs.

We might be tempted to call such folk *zombies* – they act like us, and we can't distinguish them from us from outside, but inside, they are empty.[4]

Richard Rorty anticipates the worry that functionalist accounts of action or linguistic output must leave something out. He contends that there is something right about this sort of worry, but it is something that functionalists can accommodate. What gets left out, presumably, is that private, inner, direct element of consciousness. But we *do* have linguistic analogues of that: when you're having one of those special episodes, you're the only one who gets to say what it's like. And so, we have linguistic rules that reflect that. Rorty notes that 'incorrigibility is the mark of the mental', in that you are the final arbiter of what you assent to, what you say you believe, or what you're feeling right now (Rorty 1970). So instead of not reflecting that interiority of the mind, Rorty's linguistic theory of mental content is *designed to capture it* as a functional feature of our language. What more, the functionalist may say, could you want?

A further worry about pragmatist functionalism is that it fails to reflect the definite ways in which our beliefs represent the world. When someone believes that something is *triangular*, she takes it that the thing is shaped in such and such a way. But what is the way so conceived? One may say that triangles are closed figures with three sides, or closed figures with three angles, or closed figures composed of straight lines connecting three nonlinear points. Triangles are conceived under *distinct descriptions*, but the way we treat them and to what the descriptions apply are all *the same*. Moreover, if someone just has the ability to distinguish triangles from things that aren't triangles, it doesn't follow that she is doing so because she sees them *as triangles* under any description.

So functionalist-pragmatist takes on beliefs and their content risk not respecting the specificity of content or perhaps content at all. The view treats the proposed content differences as ones that do not matter, and treats the actional output as the final arbiter of meaning. However, this is surely contentious and perhaps backward, since what matters from the inside is the belief and how one takes the world. If the pragmatist holds that such differences in how one takes the world as differences that don't matter, then instead of this being a reason to reject one's view of the interiority of belief's content, it may be a reason to reject pragmatism as too sloppy to respect content.[5]

PRAGMATISM AND METAPHYSICS

PRAGMATISM AND INDIVIDUALS

Things

A common thought is that the world is composed of *things*. Of these things, there are rocks, possums, trees, and people. There are additionally *collections* of things, like rock bands, piles, teams, and confederations. The intuition behind distinguishing these two classes is that with collections, we see them merely as groupings of individual things. With individual things, however, they are unto themselves. They can be apart from one another and still be their own things.

The crucial element of things is their separability – they aren't so dependent on each other for their individual existence that you can't take one away without taking the other away. Rocks and possums are separate things, since if you take some rock away, even the one the possum is sitting on, the possum will still be itself (just without a rock to sit on). The same goes for the rock. Take away the possum, and the rock is still there. However, with some other things, they aren't separable. Take the car in the parking lot with the scratch on it. If you take the scratch away, the car is still there, but if you take the car away, the scratch can't still be there. Think of the nonsense of *Alice in Wonderland* with the Cheshire cat's grin hanging about after the cat is gone – things like scratches and grins just aren't like that.

There is a standard distinction between *objects* and their *properties*. Objects are things in that robust and independent sense of being separable, and properties are things that depend in some way or other on their objects. Aristotle distinguished between *substances* and their *properties* on this basis and even noted that there is a functional linguistic basis for the division, since substances, properly conceived, can never be properties of other substances. That is, your car, for example, has many properties, and those properties can be said of other cars, too. Your car, perhaps, is red, and it may be said of other cars that they are red, too. However, other cars are not said to be your car (that specific one). They can be your car's color, your car's shape, or your car's age, but so long as they are *other* cars, they are not that specific one that is your car. You may buy them and make them *your cars* (in that you now own them), but you cannot by buying one car (x) make it into another car (y).

This commonsense picture of the world occasions some puzzles. One is about how things maintain their identity over time. Take your car, again. Imagine that every day, you go to the auto parts store and buy just one replacement part for your car. You bring it home and replace the correlate part in your car and leave the old part in a corner of your garage. After a few years, you find you've replaced *every* part of your car. You then take the pile of old parts in the corner and build a new car out of them. Which one is the original car? It seems that if you progressively replace parts over the years, the car is still the same car. Even once you've replaced all the parts, it is still the same car. But now that the old parts are reassembled, we have a problem. Many people's thoughts are conflicted on these issues, and this is because with the car, we have things with parts progressively replaced. In one way the car is an individual thing, but in another way, it is a mere collection of smaller, more basic parts. The problem arises because we think that small, progressive changes in the parts do not destroy the identity of the whole individual thing. When small changes add up, we have no principled reason to say where we draw the line with identity.

Perhaps the whole notion of an individual thing is an error. Maybe thinking of objects in terms of separate things from the properties is the problem? Maybe there is no extra thing, object, or substance. There are just bundles of properties. Call this view *nihilism* or *the bundle theory.*

Others say the lesson of this puzzle is not that there is no such thing as individuals, but that we are looking on the wrong level – there are not *many* things, but *one* thing making various changes. The view is sometimes called *monism*. Recall the coherence theory of truth, taking all facts to fit together in one whole, and the whole determines whether facts fit or not. The analogy was a jigsaw puzzle. Monism is a species of this view, one that holds that there is *really* only one thing: the puzzle.

A good deal of Western metaphysics has been posited on the various exchanges between the three options of metaphysical pluralism (there are lots of different objects), nihilism (there are no objects), and monism (there is just one object). Nihilism's biggest problem, of course, is dealing with the intuition that drives the notion of an object (you can't have properties without them). Monism's basic problem is being able to answer the very powerful intuition that possums, Alpha Centauri, and the Westernmost column of the Parthenon are all separate things. Pluralism's problem is with being able to make sense of all the different things and their various changes.

Sometimes a little metaphysics makes a mess of things. Now the question is whether *more* metaphysics will fix things rather than make things even worse. On this matter, most pragmatists hold that the evidence points to the breakdown of metaphysics as traditionally construed. Metaphysics needs reconstruction.

James on Monism and Pluralism

James employed his pragmatic criterion for resolving philosophical disputes by asking what were the practical differences between holding that monism or pluralism was true (he did not address the bundle theory). From one perspective, it seems little hangs on how one comes down on the matter when it comes to crossing the street. Whether you think you and a bus are part of one big object or not, not being hit by it is nevertheless preferable. However, James argues, there is a difference between the monism and pluralism in terms of how one sees things and people as autonomous. If one is a monist, one views all things as deeply tied together (again, monism entails the doctrine of internal relations, from Chapter 2), and as a consequence, one would view resistance to the collectivity of things as irrational. Pluralism requires that one see things, if together, as loosely tied and independent. James makes a political analogy: 'The pluralistic world is like a federal republic than like an empire or a kingdom' (1996: 321–2).

Monism forces us to see the whole as complete and as what must be maintained. Pluralism sees the unities as momentary and perhaps fleeting. See the difference, perhaps, in views on marriage – if one sees husband and wife as a unity instead of as cooperating and loving persons, one will view the decision to dissolve the marriage differently. Monism risks what James calls 'inner rigidity' (WWJ, 270). James reasons that since pluralism is in the service of liberty, it leaves us with tasks to take on, since the coordination of things is incomplete, it is the preferred option (1996: 329). However, one cannot be a pure pluralist – there nevertheless are unities to be preserved and we need to work out the proper places for ourselves in this world. James takes it, then, that one cannot be an absolute monist nor an absolute pluralist. Instead, he holds it that because the world is 'imperfectly unified . . . and perhaps always to remain so . . . pragmatism must turn its back on absolute monism, and follow pluralism's more empirical path' (WWJ, 269).

Monists object that this take on the situation and its ethical-political consequences begs the question. F. H. Bradley, one of James's regular philosophical interlocutors, denies the independent existence of selves. Why, if there are not *real* selves, should we promote their freedom? If they are modifications of the single unity of reality, they should *fit in* and *play their roles*, not be given free reign. In fact, if one sees things from the proper perspective, the responsible (and hence truly free) action is one done in accord with the whole and its structure (1963/1922: 679). According to Bradley, to claim that monism crushes *freedom* is to misconstrue the term.

Events and Process Metaphysics

Another puzzling thing about things is that we often think that events like concerts, wars, speeches, and years are things. Additionally, there is the same commonsense dependence of the event's properties on them as that of the properties of physical things (i.e., you can't have the property without the thing – no loudness of the concert unless there's a concert to begin with). However, we are not inclined to think of events as *objects* or *substances*, as extra things to which properties attach. We are more inclined to think of events as *processes*, things that arise relationally over time, comprised of a confluence of activities that give rise to the properties.

Given that the notion of a *process* is such a neat answer to the puzzle of events, a number of American philosophers reasoned that it may solve the larger problem of metaphysics of individuals. The thought, really, is an old one. Heraclitus had claimed that everything is flux, and though this flux is ever-changing, it nevertheless is governed by laws (Kirk and Raven 1962: Fragments 197 and 220).

Alfred North Whitehead's *Process and Reality* was designed both to capture the processes of change that constituted reality and to account for the laws that govern these changes. Think, perhaps, of process philosophy as an application of functionalism (the view that a mental state is to be defined in terms of what it does) to all things.

The problem with a metaphysics of things as objects or substances is that we try to extract things from events. For example, a sunrise consists of, on the standard view, the sun (the thing) rising (having progressive relational properties of distance from the horizon).[6] However, what we *really* have is an *event*, and though objects and their various relations may be extracted from them in thought, they are only useful ways of talking about structural relations between one event and other events (other sunrises, sunsets, midday, and so on). What the processes have are structural elements that distinguish them or make them similar, and this allows them to be reidentifiable and also to integrate with each other intelligibly. Whitehead's categories for these structures are those of *concrescence* (when things come together), which produces what he calls *actual occasions*. Everything that is, on the process view, is a coming together of a number of separate but concurrent processes (1929: 18). Events, however, come apart or end. But they do not end forever, as other processes begin anew. Whitehead calls these *prehensions*, which are transitions between actual occasions, their completion, and the beginnings of new processes. In a sense, prehensions are the future possibilities of events; they are what they portend, what ground they break, and what new ideas they give us (1929: 32). Finally, a group of actual occasions is called a *nexus*, where the prehensions of those actual occasions develop between themselves to produce further actual occasions.

A long-standing objection to the process view is that the individual things we think we know and can notice at one time and then recognize again later have dropped out entirely. P. F. Strawson famously posed a version of the objection: If we see the basic unit of reality as the event or occurrence, then Socrates wasn't really a *thing*, but a continuous bit of *Socratizing*. When we talk about the lightbulb in a library reading lamp, we aren't talking about an individual substance or object, but a process of lightbulbing there inside what is librarying. But with each of these, *that* person Socrates, *that* lightbulb, *that* library all seem to be the objects we know things about. We know of Socrates that he is dead. Not that there is no more Socratizing. We know of the lightbulb that it is burnt out, and we know of the library that it is on 4th street. Process metaphysics, then, makes a hash out of our knowledge of discrete individual things, since when we know something about the lightbulb, we seem to know something about the object named, not about processes located amongst other processes (Strawson 1959: 36–7).

Carnapian and Goodmanian Pragmatism

Rudolf Carnap's and Nelson Goodman's response to the metaphysical issue of the basic elements of reality is to note that it regularly depends on what one plans on doing with one's theory of reality.

That is, we employ metaphysical theories to direct our practices or other theorizing, and our choice of metaphysics should be determined by how well it fits with the practices or theorizing we plan to use it in.

Carnap's argument focuses on the logics and linguistic frameworks one takes to be fundamental or correct about reality's basic building blocks. However, one cannot reason to any definitive conclusion about this because the question as to what it is for something to be (or be a something) is a question *internal* to a language or logic. The question as to which language or logic is right is one that is *external* to the language or logic; it is a question that cannot be resolved because it is not framed within the language (1967/1950: 73). Instead, we should see our metaphysics and the linguistic forms that attend them as tools for coping with reality, developing theories that anticipate and control the future. Languages that allow us these benefits are the ones we should prefer, and sometimes it may be that we need an event ontology in one case and an object–substance ontology in another. We need to recognize, Carnap holds, that these theories are just conglomerations of words, linguistic artifacts we use. As a consequence, Carnap concludes:

> The acceptance or rejection of abstract linguistic forms, just as the acceptance of any other linguistic forms in any branch of science, will finally be decided by their efficacy as instruments. (1967/1950: 83)

The test of a theory of reality is not how well it is defended in arguments with its competitors, but whether it outperforms them. Some metaphysics are useful, and we may use them. Other metaphysical theories are futile, and they are as good as false to us. The question now is how well these theories live up to their promises.

Nelson Goodman's similar strategy embraces the variety of takes on the world, and he takes it that with the present issue, 'identity or constancy in a world is identity with respect to what is within that world as organized' (1978: 8). Here, Goodman ventures further than the Carnapian account of languages and logics of the world. Goodman is talking about *worlds*, each with its own reality relative to a thinker's purposes for which it has been made:

Ironically . . . our passion for one world is satisfied, at different times and for different purposes, in different ways. Not only motion, derivation, weighing, order, but even reality is relative. That right versions and actual worlds are many does not obliterate the distinction between right and wrong versions, does not recognize merely possible worlds answering to wrong versions, and does not imply that all right alternatives are equally good for every or indeed for any purpose. (1978: 21–2)

The crucial thing, Goodman notes, is not to be too taken with this notion that there are multitudes of made worlds each right for its own purposes and criticizable only from inside. What is important is crafting the right world for current needs, developing a vocabulary to address our standing concerns:

Mere acknowledgement of the many available frames of reference provides us with no map of the motions of the heavenly bodies . . . awareness of varied ways of seeing paints no pictures. A broad mind is no substitute for hard work. (1978: 22)

The point of the world-making thesis is not just that of prohibiting criticism across worlds, but to spur further innovation in developing new ones. Again, Carnap's and Goodman's theses are similar in that both take questions of the adequacy of ontologies to be internal to the ontologies, and that the means of deciding between competing ontologies is their practical value. They agree there is no external perspective from which to adjudge. Carnap's emphasis is on now turning to evaluating the ontologies in terms of their relative success as vocabularies that direct action or further scientific work. Goodman's emphasis is that these worlds are not complete, and he exhorts us not to just test the ones we have but to constantly develop new ones.

The core of Carnapian ontological and Goodmanian world-making pragmatism is the distinction between internal and external views regarding questions of adequacy. There are varieties of ways to see the world, talk about it, and live in it. However, the stark prohibition of external questions takes the point too far. In fact, the distinction is self-defeating. Here is how. If we say one theoretical language (L1) and another language (L2) are different solutions to the same problem, we must identify some problem that shares an identity across the two languages. In our case, the metaphysics of individuals is the problem. This, presumably, requires that we are using a third language (L3) that in which such an identity of a problem can be formulated. Once we see things from this perspective, questions about the adequacy of L1 or L2 to the task may be *external to them*, but it is nevertheless *internal to L3*. The point here is that any time we can recognize a disagreement between two languages, conceptual schemes, or worlds, we see that they must share some broader language, conceptual scheme, or world for them to disagree over the same thing.

Donald Davidson argues for this point, noting that

> [d]ifferent points of view make sense, but only if there is a common co-ordinate system on which to plot them; yet the existence of a common system belies the claim of dramatic incomparability. (1984: 184)

What follows is that, if we can countenance them, all these languages share the same conceptual space. So questions as to which of the two schemes in disagreement is right are not only meaningful, but also pressing. This point, of course, does not solve the issue between the two camps in L1 and L2. Nor does it provide the means of solving the metaphysical issues we have been struggling with. But it does remind us that some philosophical strategies block the road of inquiry.

CHAPTER 5

PRAGMATISM AND ETHICS

We have seen in preceding chapters that all versions of pragmatism are species of empiricism; additionally, we have seen that all pragmatisms endorse some style of *naturalism*. Very roughly, empiricism is the view that all knowledge has its source in experience. Naturalism is, very roughly, the view that the world investigated by empirical science is the only world there is. Naturalists reject appeals to objects, beings, or forces that are claimed to reside beyond the natural world.

We have also seen that pragmatism is also concerned with *action*. Particularly, we have seen that pragmatists are concerned to make action more successful. Indeed, the pragmatisms of Peirce, James, and Dewey identify the *purpose* of thought itself with successful action. Recall that the pragmatic maxim entails that any proposition that could have no bearing on action was meaningless; James went as far as to identify the truth of a proposition with its ability to guide action toward success.

We should expect, then, that pragmatists would be especially keen to develop a moral philosophy, an ethics. Although Peirce wrote almost nothing in ethics, moral philosophy plays a leading role in the work of James and Dewey. Subsequent pragmatists have placed normative questions at the center of their program. In this chapter, we will examine several pragmatist views of ethics. We will begin with James's meliorism. From there, we will examine Dewey's conception of moral inquiry and Hilary Putnam's recent work on the distinction between fact and value. Finally, we will discuss a pragmatic methodology prominent in contemporary ethics, namely, reflective equilibrium. Before proceeding, however, we must first confront a problem.

A PROBLEM: 'IS' AND 'OUGHT'

Perhaps the very idea of a pragmatist ethics is confused. If, as we have seen, pragmatism is a kind of naturalism, then it seeks to restrict philosophical reflection to the subject matter accessible to science. It seems obvious that science aims to discern the truth with respect to its subject matter. But discerning the truth means discovering *what is the case*. Hence scientists address questions such as At what temperature will this liquid boil? How did squid evolve? What is the structure of DNA? How old is the universe? Such questions call for answers that accurately represent the way the world is. When we ask the question, *At what temperature does this liquid boil?* we are not asking for some judgment about what temperature it would be *good* for the liquid to boil. We want to know the temperature at which it will, *in fact*, boil; we are looking for an answer of the form, *That liquid boils at 300 degrees*. Given this, we might say that science proffers *descriptions* of the world.

Now contrast statements of the form, *That liquid boils at 300 degrees*, *The structure of DNA is a double-helix*, and *The universe is 14 billion years old*, with statements of the following sort: *One should never lie*, *You ought to keep your promises*, and *Murderers deserve capital punishment*. Statements of this latter kind do not purport to *describe* the world. To see this, notice that the statement, *Murderers deserve capital punishment*, if it is true, would be true even in a world in which capital punishment was universally outlawed. This is because the statement in question does not attempt to report what *in fact* happens to murderers. Rather, the statement purports to say something about what *ought to be the case*. Very roughly, the statement says that murderers *ought* to be executed. A similar analysis is in order for the other statements above. The statement *One should never lie*, if true, would be true in a world in which lying was encouraged. This is because the statement does not attempt to report what is the case; rather, the statement claims that one *ought not* lie, or that it is *wrong* to lie.

We can capture the difference between statements like *The universe is 14 billion years old* and statements like *One should never lie* by saying that statements of the former kind are *descriptive* whereas statements of the latter kind are *prescriptive*. Descriptive statements attempt to capture *what is* the case. Prescriptive statements attempt to capture *what ought to be* the case. Accordingly, prescriptive statements, unlike descriptive statements, make *recommendations*; they propose or *prescribe* that we take certain actions and avoid others. No straightforwardly descriptive statement – no matter how accurate or well confirmed or widely agreed upon – could entail a prescription. A famous way of putting this point is that one can never derive *ought* from *is*. No descriptive statement entails a prescriptive one.

Here is the problem. Science does not speak to what *ought to be* the case, but only to what *is* the case. However, ethics is concerned fundamentally with prescriptions, statements concerning how we *ought* to behave and what *ought* to be the case. As pragmatism is committed to naturalism, and accordingly seeks to bring philosophy in line with the methods of the natural sciences, it is unclear how pragmatism could support a moral philosophy. It seems that to deal in prescriptions is necessarily to look beyond the world treated by science; consequently, any philosophy committed to naturalism must confine itself to descriptive statements, and therefore cannot devise an ethics.

Call this the *is/ought* problem. This problem forms the background to our discussion of pragmatism and ethics, and we shall be returning to it throughout this chapter. As we shall see, the pragmatist views we will consider offer different responses to the *is/ought* problem.

JAMESIAN MELIORISM

Preliminary: A Simple Ethical Egoism

One way to deal with the *is/ought* problem is to argue that prescriptive statements really just are a kind of descriptive statement. The way to do this is to maintain that familiar moral terms – *good*, *bad*, *right*, and *wrong* – can be understood as referring to empirical states of affairs. Were such a view of moral terms to succeed, it could be easily shown that prescriptive statements really just are a special variety of descriptive statement, and hence treatable by the methods employed by science. To see this, consider a straightforward view of this type, a view called *simple ethical egoism*. The simple ethical egoist contends that moral statements are to be analyzed in terms of individual preferences or *interests*. On this view, the statement *x is good* means something like *x furthers one's interests*; thus when one *asserts* that *X is good*, one asserts that one has an interest which *x* furthers. The simple ethical egoist hence holds that the statement *x is good* is a kind of description, much like *this liquid will boil at 300 degrees*.

That is, if the moral term *good* is taken to mean *interest furthering*, then statements like *x is good* are empirically verifiable predictions; one could *observe* whether in fact *x* does further one's interests and thereby determine whether in fact *x* is good.

What about the *prescriptive* nature of moral statements? The simple ethical egoist treats prescriptions as recommendations based on empirical generalizations concerning what acts *tend* to serve one's interests. Hence, the statement *One should never lie* means something like, *Lying frustrates one's interests*. Again, prescriptive statements are analyzed in terms of the empirical, and hence observable, consequences of a given act. It seems that naturalism can provide a moral theory after all. All that is required is an empirical analysis of moral terms and statements.

Of course, as its name indicates, simple ethical egoism is a highly simplified version of naturalist ethics. In fact, it is *simplistic*. It would be difficult to find any philosopher endorsing the view as we have described it. A less simple version of this kind of view would have to specify with considerable precision the idea of an *interest*, and the concept of an interest being *furthered*. Additional complications arise when one considers cases in which one's interests *conflict*, and cases in which one's interests are inconsistent with the interests of others. But we need not here take up the task of devising a more respectable ethical egoism. Our point is to call attention to a certain *strategy* in dealing with the *is/ought* problem, namely, the strategy of defining moral terms empirically and then analyzing moral statements as empirically verifiable claims about the consequences of certain actions. William James employed this strategy in developing his ethics, which we shall call *meliorism*.

Fundamentals of James's Meliorism

Jamesian meliorism begins from a premise much like that from which the simple ethical egoist begins. James claims that 'Goodness, badness, and obligation must be *realized* somewhere in order really to exist'; he then asserts that the 'only habitat' of these moral properties is 'a mind which feels them' (WWJ, 614; italic in the original). Accordingly, James analyzes moral terms as applying primarily to certain *psychological states*. He says that 'the words "good", "bad", and "obligation"' refer not to 'absolute natures' of acts but instead are 'objects of feeling and desire' that 'have no foothold or anchorage in

Being, apart from the existence of actually living minds' (WWJ, 168). Consequently, James holds that 'nothing can be good or right except so far as some consciousness feels it to be good or thinks it to be right' (WWJ, 616). To say that *x is good* is to report that someone in fact *thinks* it good, or actually *desires* it. Statements such as *x is good* are empirically verifiable; all one needs to do in order to verify that *x* is good is to find someone who actually desires *x*. James gives a similar analysis of the concept of *obligation*. A moral obligation arises, James says, only when 'some concrete person' actually makes a *claim* or a *demand* that something or other should be done (WWJ, 617). Indeed, 'The only possible reason there can be why any phenomenon ought to exist is that such a phenomenon actually is desired' (WWJ, 617). From this, James concludes that 'the essence of good is simply to satisfy demand' (WWJ, 621). Jamesian meliorism hence identifies the meaning of moral claims such as, *One ought never to lie*, as expressing a *demand* that one might make to always be told the truth; one makes such a demand on the basis of one's *desire* to not be lied to. Again, the *is/ought* problem is addressed by way of an interpretation of moral terms which identifies them with certain empirical facts. For James, the relevant facts are facts about our psychological states, primarily our desires. The good is the satisfaction of desire.

Although James's view bears certain obvious similarities with simple ethical egoism, there are crucial differences between them. Perhaps most importantly, unlike the simple ethical egoist who ties moral value to *one's own interests*, James recognizes the moral status of *any* demand, even those issued by others. Whereas the simple ethical egoist identifies the right action in any given context with that action which best furthers the interests of the agent, James acknowledges that 'every . . . claim creates in so far forth an obligation' (WWJ, 617); consequently, on James's view, the interests of others can be the source of our obligations, regardless of whether it furthers our interest to satisfy them.

In this way, James's meliorism involves an *egalitarian* component: *every demand* and *every interest*, no matter whose demand or interest it may be, morally counts. James takes this egalitarian commitment to be consistent with his naturalism: if moral terms like *good* and *bad* refer to certain psychological states – let us call them *satisfaction* and *dissatisfaction* – then it seems that it should not matter morally *which of us* is in those states. *My* dissatisfaction is, from the moral point of view, no *more* a bad than *yours*; similarly, *your* satisfaction is no less a moral good than *mine*. Hence the core of James's moral theory:

> Since everything which is demanded is by that fact a good, must not the guiding principle for ethical philosophy . . . be simply to satisfy at all times *as many demands as we can?* That act must be the best act, accordingly, which makes for the *best whole*, in the sense of awakening the least sum of dissatisfactions. (WWJ, 623; italics in the original)

We can see now why we have been calling James's view *meliorism*. The term *meliorism* derives from the Greek verb 'to care for', and, as is evident in the quotation above, the center of Jamesian morality is the effort to *improve* the total sum of satisfaction over dissatisfaction in the world, to 'act as to bring about the very largest total universe of good which we can see' (WWJ, 626).

Utilitarianism and Pluralism

Meliorism bids us to strive to satisfy as many demands – our own and those of others – as possible. For this reason, meliorism may seem to be a species of a popular moral theory known as *utilitarianism*. Very roughly, utilitarianism is the view according to which that action is morally best which, as compared with alternative actions one could perform, will produce the greatest quantity of happiness – defined as the presence of pleasure and the absence of pain – for all affected by the action. The similarities of utilitarianism to meliorism should be obvious. However, as with simple ethical egoism, there is a crucial difference between the two views that must be made explicit if we are to understand James's ethics.

A central element of utilitarianism is the commitment to a theory of value called *hedonism*. Hedonism is the view that pleasure is the only thing of *intrinsic value*. That is, hedonists hold that pleasure is the only thing that is valuable in itself. Consequently, hedonists maintain that anything other than pleasure that is valuable – such as money, health, friendship, or freedom – derives its value entirely from its tendency to generate pleasure (or at least avoid pain). For example, the value of money is clearly *instrumental*. Green pieces of paper have no value in themselves; insofar as the green pieces of paper have value at all, they have it because they are *instruments*, they can be used to buy things that will generate pleasure.

One implication of hedonism is that the value of any particular thing can be compared to the value of any other thing. That is, hedonism entails that for any two values, A and B, one could determine decisively whether A is more valuable than, less valuable than, or equally valuable to B. This is because hedonists hold that there is but one intrinsic value – pleasure – and therefore but one *scale* by which values could be compared or rank-ordered, namely, *quantity of pleasure*. Thus, every value conflict has a determinate, morally optimal resolution. Again, for any two conflicting values, A and B, it is the case that either (a) the value of A is greater than that of B, or (b) the value of A is less than that of B, or (c) A and B are of equal value. In the first case, the conflict is morally resolved by choosing A over B; in the second case, B should be chosen over A; and in the third, A and B are morally equivalent options, so there is no moral contest between them after all.

One difficulty concerns the plausibility of this aspect of hedonism. Does it really make sense to think of all values as comparable on a single scale? Consider: The hedonist holds that friendship and money are both *instrumental* values. This means that love and money are both valuable only insofar as they tend to produce or promote pleasure. Hence the hedonist is committed to the view that there is some sum of money that is equivalent to the value of love. If there's a sum of money that is equivalent in value to love, then there's another sum of money that *exceeds* the value of love. Hence money and love are *exchangeable*. Money *can* buy love.

But this seems to be a mistake. To be sure, we are accustomed to think that money *cannot* buy love. Notice, however, that the thought that money cannot buy love is *not* the thought that love is *too expensive*. Rather, we think that money cannot buy love because *there could be no sum of money that would be equal in value to love*. This is because we tend to think that money and love are values of *fundamentally different kinds*. That is, we tend to think that money and love are *incommensurable* – there is no common scale of value by means of which love and money can be compared. Accordingly, when confronted with a situation in which we must choose between love and money – as when, say, one is offered a very high-paying job in a distant city, and relocation would require one to abandon a budding romance – we feel at a loss. More importantly, it seems clear that the conflict cannot be resolved by rank-ordering the quantities of pleasure associated with each option. In such cases, it is not clear *what* to do, but something must be done. We often characterize such cases as *tragic*.

Although James bids us to satisfy 'as many demands as we can' (WWJ, 623), he is not a utilitarian; the theory of value underlying meliorism is not hedonism. James rejects the central hedonist claim that there is but one intrinsic value; likewise, he rejects the related thesis that all goods are commensurable. To put the matter in a slightly different way, James rejects hedonism for being a *monistic* theory of value, and adopts a view of value called *pluralism*. We saw in Chapter 4 that *pluralism* in metaphysics is the view that there are different *things*. Analogously, the vale pluralist denies that there is a single intrinsic value to which all other values are reducible, and thus denies that there is a common measure by means of which different goods can be rank-ordered. Instead, the pluralist countenances 'an exuberant mass of goods with which human nature is in travail', and holds that 'there is hardly a good which we can imagine except as competing for the possession of the same bit of space and time with some other imagined good' (WWJ, 622).

Thus the pluralist denies that every moral conflict admits of a single morally optimal resolution. In fact, the pluralist claims that some moral conflicts are such that *no* morally comfortable resolution is possible. As our case of the high-paying job and the budding romance suggests, sometimes we are faced with a moral decision between two undeniable goods where something must be done, but every option involves a sacrifice of some good. The important point is that in such cases, there is no third value to which someone may appeal in deciding how to choose between the high-paying job and the budding romance. For the pluralist, nothing plays the role that pleasure plays in hedonism; the pluralist contends that there is no *summum bonum* in light of which conflicts can be resolved. Thus moral choice is frequently tragic: we must choose between incommensurable goods, without the guidance of reason or principles, and we inevitably suffer a moral loss. As James explains, 'there is always a *pinch* between the ideal and the actual which can only be got through by leaving part of the ideal behind' (WWJ, 621; italic in the original).

Problems with Meliorism

We now consider some objections to meliorism. First, consider James's view that 'everything which is demanded is by that fact a good'

(WWJ, 623). It is worth noting that James arrives at this view by way of his claim that to call something good is to say that someone in fact demands it. But it simply does not follow from James's premise that 'nothing can be good or right except so far as some consciousness feels it to be good or thinks it to be right' (WWJ, 616) that 'everything which is demanded is by that fact a good' (WWJ, 623). We can grant that whatever is good is good because someone in fact desires it without thereby committing to the claim that whatever anyone in fact desires is *ipso facto* a good. The former does not entail the latter.

We need not dwell on the failure of this inference. Perhaps James simply means to assert both that (a) *if x is good, then it is demanded* and (b) *if x is demanded, then it is good*. We can understand why James is keen to assert the latter: James's pluralism *requires* that the fact that someone demands *x* is sufficient for the good of *x*. Were James to hold that there is some *other* requirement that *x* must meet if it is to be a good, James would be well on his way toward providing a *monist* theory of value, a theory according to which all goods share some property in common. But recall that this is exactly what the pluralist denies. To repeat, according to the pluralist, *all that is required for x to be a good is simply that x satisfy a demand*. James adds that 'The demand may be for anything under the sun' because the ideals on the basis of which we issue demands have 'no common character apart from the fact that they are ideals' (WWJ, 621).

How plausible is this? It seems obvious that some demands should not be met. The demands of the thief, the addict, the cheat, and the tyrant are clear examples. Should we seek to satisfy such demands? Now, James could argue that the demand of, say, the tyrant ought not be satisfied because the tyrant's demand is *too costly* given the overall economy of demands in the world. In fact, James asserts that 'those ideals must be written highest which *prevail at the least cost*, or by whose realization the least possible number of other ideals are destroyed' (WWJ, 623; italic in the original). Hence James would reply that in order to realize the tyrant's ideal we would have to sacrifice too many other ideals. Thus it is permissible to leave the tyrant dissatisfied.

But this reply misses the point. One could insist that the reason why we may justifiably dismiss the tyrant's demands is not that they conflict with other, more easily realized demands, but rather because the tyrant makes demands that it would be *immoral* to meet. One insists that we can morally evaluate demands independently of the costs (to other demands) of realizing them.

Consider a different kind of case. Let us imagine Robin Hood's more discerning sister, Betty Hood. Whereas Robin Hood steals from the rich and gives to the poor, Betty Hood steals only from the *super rich* and gives to the poor. Let us also stipulate that someone is *super rich* only if one could be the victim of Betty's thievery without sustaining any dissatisfaction. That is, Betty Hood steals only from those who are so rich that they will not notice the loss. Betty's activities therefore help to satisfy the demands of the poor – she gives them the money that she steals from the super rich – and they do nothing to frustrate the demands of the super rich, for their lives go on just as they otherwise would. It seems, then, that James could have no objection to Betty's activities; in fact, James might have to take the stronger view that Betty's actions are morally right, and possibly obligatory.

Can this be correct? The fact that Betty steals from people who will not miss the money and then gives that money to the needy seems irrelevant to the morality of the situation. Betty Hood's activities are morally wrong *simply because they are instances of stealing*, and stealing is wrong no matter whom one steals from. We might insist against James that the wrongness of stealing is independent of some calculation of the *cost* of stealing in the overall economy of demands.

There is a lot more to say. However, it is clear that there are certain commonsense moral commitments that meliorism cannot accommodate. We think that tyranny, theft, and dishonesty, are wrong regardless of the costs of satisfying the demands of the tyrant, thief, and liar. We tend to think that certain demands are *in themselves* immoral. This is because we tend to think that certain moral claims – for example, to freedom, property, and honesty – are valid regardless of who demands what.

A related difficulty looms. James holds that we should 'act so as to bring about the very largest total universe of good which we can see' (WWJ, 626). As we have seen, his pluralism entails that x, y, and z could all be goods without having anything at all in common other than that for each there is some person who desires them. It follows, then, that the 'largest total universe of good' is the universe in which the greatest number of demands is met. So the core prescription of James's ethics is: act so as to satisfy as many demands as possible. Indeed, James advises us more generally to 'invent some manner of realizing your own ideals which will also satisfy the alien demands' (WWJ, 623).

This overlooks the fact that certain kinds of ideals are such that to hold them is necessarily to judge certain other ideals to be immoral and thus unworthy of realization (Nagel 2001: 107). Not all moral conflict is due to an overall lack of resources or a general inability to accommodate everyone. Some conflict is due to the fact that some moral commitments involve a *rejection*, or even a *refusal*, of other moral commitments. The most obvious example of this kind of commitment is religious belief. Certain forms of religious belief are such that their proponents must see those who hold different religious commitments as not simply committed to a different ideal, but as committed to an ideal that is mistaken, dangerous, ignorant, or evil. For example, certain forms of fundamentalist Christianity hold that Hindus are not simply following a different religion, but rather are pursuing a *false* religion. To adopt this form of Christianity is necessarily to judge the Hindu ideal to be *idolatrous* since it does not recognize (or perhaps positively denies) the divinity of Jesus Christ. To say, with James, to this kind of Christian that she should try to practice her Christianity in a way 'which will also satisfy' (WWJ, 623) the Hindu demands is to say to the Christian that she must regard the Hindu ideal as an ideal *worthy* of accommodation. But this is precisely what she cannot do; to regard the Hindu demand as worth satisfying is to commit an act of blasphemy, and thus to violate her own ideal.

As this kind of case shows, when we are dealing with certain kinds of moral conflict, we are confronted not just with conflicting demands, but with conflicting views of what is morally acceptable. Again, James bids us to act so as to bring about 'the very largest total universe of goods' (WWJ, 626). But we are often divided precisely over the question of which states of affairs should count as good; thus the injunction to bring about 'the very largest total universe of goods' is nearly vacuous. To return to the example above, the Christian believes that a world in which no Hindu demands are satisfied is a world with more goods in it than a world in which the Hindu ideal flourishes. Our Christian, then, should act so as to bring about a *reduction* in the number of Hindus. Perhaps there are certain radical Hindus who hold that Christianity is a wrong-headed and immoral ideal. Following James, we should say that the racial Hindus have good reason to act so as to bring about a reduction in the number of Christians in the world. Both the fundamentalist Christians and the radical Hindus seem to be acting in accordance with the meliorist prescription, but the result is a state of war between the conflicting parties. It is difficult to see how a state of affairs in which rival factions are at war actually contributes to making a better world.

Hence we confront a final difficulty. Recall that the pluralist wants to deny that there is a single or uniform essence of *good*. That is, according to the pluralist, any good thing is good only in that someone desires it. Yet it seems clear that some of our desires entail desires that others' desires *not* be met. What is needed to prevent a state of war of the sort mentioned above is a substantive conception of toleration, one which prescribes that we ought to tolerate some of those who embrace ideals that are not merely *different from* our own, but are, from our point of view, not *moral* ideals at all. Such an account would prescribe that we ought to tolerate certain others even when it frustrates our own ideals to do so. But this kind of account of the value of toleration would have to identify the value of toleration *outside* of the existing economy of desires and demands. As we have seen, James is committed to the thesis that *there is no such thing* as a good that is not in fact demanded by some person. Accordingly, he cannot supply the kind account of toleration that is called for.

MORAL METHODISM

The Jamesian meliorist attempts to escape the *is/ought* problem by interpreting moral statements as special kinds of descriptions; recall that, on James's view, moral terms refer to psychological states of satisfaction and dissatisfaction and moral judgments are empirical generalizations about which actions will bring about these states. According to James *there is nothing more to something being good than the fact the someone or other in fact desires it*. But it is just this commitment that renders James unable to make the kind of principled case for toleration that his meliorism demands. Hence it seems that the strategy for dealing with the *is/ought* problem – namely, the strategy of treating prescriptions as a kind of description – fails. A different strategy is needed.

John Dewey and, more recently, Hilary Putnam have proposed a different kind of pragmatist approach to ethics. On their view, ethical theory should begin not with a naturalist analysis of the meaning of moral terms, but with an examination of *method*. Specifically, Dewey and Putnam propose a *method of moral inquiry*; they contend that *what we do* when confronted with moral problems is the fundamental issue for moral theory. They hold that once we get clear on our methodology, the remainder of moral theory – including the analysis of moral terms – will fall into place. As we will see, the Dewey/Putnam approach attempts to address the *is/ought* problem by collapsing the distinction between description and prescription. But in collapsing the distinction, they do not attempt, with James, to *translate* prescriptive statements into descriptive ones; rather, Dewey and Putnam seek to deny that statements can be categorized as either descriptive or prescriptive. That is, they deny the Jamesian view that prescriptive statements are a kind of descriptive statement because they refuse to adopt the prescription/description distinction in the first place. Since, as we have said, the focus of this kind of pragmatist view is the method of dealing with moral problems, we call the Dewey/Putnam proposal *moral methodism*. We begin with a sketch of methodism and then turn to the way in which the methodist treats the *is/ought* problem.

Inquiry and Valuation

In our sketch of Dewey's pragmatism in Chapter 1, we emphasized the role of inquiry in his philosophical system. Indeed, it is not too far off the mark to say that at the core of Dewey's pragmatism is a commitment to the idea that getting a proper understanding of inquiry is essential to making philosophical progress of any kind. This is why Dewey, in his more programmatic works such as *Reconstruction in Philosophy* (MW12) and the essays 'The Need for a Recovery of Philosophy' (MW10) and 'The Influence of Darwinism on Philosophy' (MW4), fixes on questions of method; in fact, his criticism of traditional approaches to philosophy is that these approaches employ a methodology that is, according to Dewey, flawed because it is insufficiently empirical.

The methodist proposal, then, is that ethics can be brought under the scope of an empirical method of inquiry. In fact, both Dewey and Putnam contend that questions and problems of ethics should be approached *with the very same method of inquiry* employed in empirical science. Putnam summarizes the stance of moral methodism succinctly, 'What holds for good inquiry in general holds for value inquiry in particular' (2002: 104). So let us again turn, then, to Dewey's general theory of inquiry.

To review quickly material from Chapter 1: Dewey follows Peirce in holding that inquiry commences in response to a problem. Although Peirce characterized the stimulus to inquiry as the feeling of doubt, Dewey contends that inquiry is instigated by confrontation with a *problematic situation*. By *situation* Dewey means 'not a single object of event' but the 'contextual whole' or experience (LW12: 72; italic in the original). A situation is *problematic* when it is 'uncertain, unsettled, [and] disturbed' (LW12: 109). Inquiry, then, is the activity of bringing order or restoring equilibrium to a problematic situation; to simplify, but only slightly, inquiry is for Dewey problem solving.

Of course, inquiry is not on Dewey's view a simple algorithm or recipe for solving problems. It is easy to see why inquiry could *not* be formalized in this way: there is an irreducible diversity of kinds of problematic situations, and no two problematic situations are identical. However, Dewey holds that all proper inquiry instantiates a common general pattern (LW12: 105), which he summarizes as follows:

(1) Perplexity, confusion, doubt, due to the fact that one is implicated in an incomplete situation whose full character is not yet determined;

(2) A conjectural anticipation – a tentative interpretation of the given elements, attributing to them a tendency to effect certain consequences;

(3) A careful survey (examination, inspection, exploration, analysis) of all attainable considerations which will define and clarify the problem at hand;

(4) A consequent elaboration of the tentative hypothesis to make it more precise and more consistent, because squaring it with a wider range of facts;

(5) Taking one stand upon the projected hypothesis as a plan of action which is applied to the existing state of affairs: doing something overtly to bring out the anticipated result, and thereby testing the hypothesis (MW9: 157).

From this, we see that, according to Dewey, inquiry is always *experimental* and success is never guaranteed. It is important to see that inquiry culminates in a *judgment* upon which one *acts*. The consequences of this act will determine whether inquiry has culminated in a restored situation, or needs to be further engaged. If the latter, one is confronted with a *new* confusion ('Well, *that* didn't work!'), and therefore one needs to go back to the drawing board to formulate a new hypothesis to test.

It should be obvious that Dewey's general theory of inquiry draws its inspiration from what we commonly call the *scientific method*. This is no accident. Dewey thought that modern experimental science provided the paradigm of proper inquiry. He went so far as to associate any cognitive process which fit this general pattern with intelligence itself. That is, according to Dewey, what it is to be *intelligent* is to employ experimental method when confronted with a problem – indeed, *any* problem at all.

Since a *situation* is the 'contextual whole' of our experience at a given moment, situations involve not only physical objects and mechanical forces, but also social factors, including habits, customs, and values. There are situations, then, which feature *disordered* values and are therefore *morally* problematic (LW13: 221). Dewey says that because such situations are marked by 'conflicting desires and alternate apparent goods' there must be 'judgment and choice' prior to action; in such cases 'what is needed is to find the right course of action, the right good' (MW12: 173).

The methodist proposal, then, is that we should approach moral problems in the same way in which we approach problems of other kinds – in other words, we should be *experimental*. This means that, when confronted with a morally problematic situation, we should follow the process roughly characterized above: We observe and clarify the problematic features of the situation; we survey available responses, forecasting likely consequences of each; we formulate a hypothesis concerning which available response will best resolve the problem; and, finally, we act and see whether the envisioned consequences match the actual ones, and, more importantly, whether we could *live* with the actual results.

Now, it is important to bear in mind that the methodist concedes that all inquiry occurs against a background of values. We value a wide array of things, experiences, and states of affairs: possessions, pleasure, health, friendships, works of art, liberty, and so on. As we have said, a *morally* problematic situation is one in which our values come into conflict, and we must decide among the things that we value which are the most *valuable*. Consequently, Dewey admits a distinction between what we in fact value and what is valuable.

Unlike James, who, as we have seen, can draw no distinction between what we desire and what we *ought* to desire, Dewey holds that 'the fact that something is desired only raises the *question* of its desirability; it does not settle it' (LW4: 208; italic in the original). The difference, according to Dewey, between the *valued* (or *desired*) and the *valuable* (or *desirable*) is that the *valuable* is that which has been *appraised* to be of value (MW8: 26); the difference, that is, is something like *reflective endorsement*. To put the contrast otherwise, the *valuable* is that which can be regarded as having value *in light of* inquiry; the *valued* is that which is in fact held to be valuable, reflectively or not.

Hence we see that the methodist sees morality as a 'continuing process, not a fixed achievement' (MW14: 194). Specifically, it is the process of confronting morally problematic situations *intelligently*, that is, experimentally. For the methodist, the moral life, then, is not a life in which certain kinds of psychological states, such as pleasure, are frequently realized; rather, the moral life is the life of cultivating by means of practice the skills involved in moral inquiry. Hence Dewey identified the 'only moral end' as *growth* (MW12: 181).

Methodism and the *Is/Ought* Problem

We shall say a bit more about growth in the next chapter. For now, let us return to the *is/ought* problem. Dewey notes that 'the idea of actively adopting experimental method in social affairs . . . strikes many as a surrender of all standards and regulative authority' (LW4: 218). This reaction is due to the intuitive pull of the distinction we introduced above between *descriptive* and *prescriptive* statements. Recall that we appealed there to a straightforward difference between sentences such as *This liquid will boil at 300 degrees* and *One should never lie*. It seemed to us that the empirical method employed by the natural scientist could examine only sentences of the first kind; science, we thought, could tell us only *what is*, not what *ought to be*. Thus Dewey's proposal that ethical questions should be addressed by the empirical methods of the sort employed in the natural sciences is, indeed, likely to strike us as deeply confused: scientific inquiry might tell us what we, in fact, do or what we, in fact, value, but no amount of scientific inquiry could tell us what we *ought* to do or value.

Now we see why moral methodism involves a *denial* of the distinction between descriptive and prescriptive statements, between fact and value: if such a distinction stands, moral methodism *is, indeed, a confused doctrine*. It is no wonder, then, that Hilary Putnam has focused so much attention on denying the 'fact/value dichotomy' (2002). But it is one thing merely to deny a seemingly commonsense distinction, and quite another to show why it should be abandoned. So we need to look at Putnam's arguments.

One thing that we need to point out before turning to Putnam's arguments is that what the methodist must deny is the *strict dichotomy* of fact and value. That is, the methodist may concede that it makes sense to treat certain statements as descriptive and others are prescriptive. What the methodist must deny is that these two categories are *exclusive* of one another, that any meaningful statement must fall on exactly one side of the supposed divide between fact and value. As Putman put it, 'a distinction is not a dichotomy' (2002: 9). Accordingly, Putnam insists that facts and values are inextricably 'entangled' (2002: 34). In what follows, then, we shall refer to Putnam's *entanglement thesis*. Why should we accept it?

The Entanglement Thesis

Putnam offers two kinds of argument for the entanglement thesis. One is a historical argument, the other is philosophical. The historical argument has it that the fact/value dichotomy is a child of another seemingly intuitive dichotomy, namely, the analytic/synthetic. Putnam alleges that the analytic/synthetic dichotomy has been undermined by Quine in his famous essay on 'Two Dogmas of Empiricism' (Quine 1961) and concludes that therefore the fact/value dichotomy is without justification (Putman 2002: 30). The analytic/synthetic dichotomy can be captured by noting the seemingly obvious difference between statements like *All bachelors are unmarried* and statements like *The current president of the United States is right-handed*. We are tempted to say of the first sentence something like, 'it is true in virtue of the *meanings* of the words "bachelor" and "unmarried"'; in the case of the second, we are likely to say that its truth depends not on the meanings of the words it contains, but on the facts, on what is the case in the world. Philosophers frequently characterize statements of the first sort (namely, those that seem true in virtue of the meaning of the words they contain) as *analytic*, and statements of the second sort (namely, true due to the facts in the world) as *synthetic*. Prior to Quine, philosophers were almost uniformly committed to the idea that every meaningful statement is either analytic or synthetic; hence the analytic/synthetic dichotomy.

The Quinean argument against this dichotomy runs that the very idea of 'true in virtue of meaning' that lies at the heart of the concept of analyticity is unclear. To wit: what does it mean to say that *All bachelors are unmarried* is true by virtue of the *meanings* of 'bachelor' and 'unmarried'? Perhaps one would say that *bachelor* and *unmarried man* (or *unmarried person?*) are *synonyms*. But it is hard to make sense of synonymy without making reference to the idea of *sameness of meaning*, and thus to *meaning*. But *meaning* is what we were trying to explicate, so the appeal to synonymy makes no progress. Perhaps, then, we might say that the terms 'bachelor' and 'unmarried man' are *substitutable* for one another, such that any sentence containing the one term could be rewritten substituting the other without changing the meaning of the sentence. But this, again, makes reference to *meaning*, the very concept we are trying to provide an analysis of. We might then say that *bachelor* 'contains' the idea of *unmarriedness*. But 'containment' is clearly a metaphor, and thus does not get us any closer to understanding the idea of a sentence being 'true by virtue of meaning'. The Quinean argument has it that this exercise could go on and on without ever reaching a point at which 'true in virtue of meaning' is made clear.

We could go further and say similar things about the synthetic side of the dichotomy. Recall that synthetic statements seem to be made true by facts in the world. Again, this seems natural enough, until we ask what, precisely, we mean by *facts*. Recall the difficulties in metaphysics between pluralists and monists regarding these matters. Just how many facts are referenced by the statement *The current president of the United States is right-handed?* Is there one fact? Or are there two facts: the fact that George W. Bush is the current president *and* the fact that George W. Bush is right-handed? Is the fact that George W. Bush is the current president the *same* fact as the fact that George W. Bush won the 2004 election? And what makes something a *fact*, anyway? Is it that it can be observed or experienced? What then of statements about electrons, germs, subatomic particles, and gravitational fields? Things only get more complicated when we consider statements concerning the past or the future. It seems,

PRAGMATISM AND ETHICS

then, that the notion of a fact that is crucial to the idea of a synthetic statement is also in need of clarification. We are not able here to fill in the further details of Quine's argument. Our point has been to suggest that the seemingly obvious difference between analytic and synthetic statements is not so obvious after all; accordingly, the thought that every meaningful statement is either analytic or synthetic is jeopardized. Putnam claims that the analytic/synthetic and fact/value dichotomies rely on the same oversimplified view of facts. Accordingly, he contends that once we see, in the case of the analytic/synthetic dichotomy, that there is no *clear* notion of fact' (2002: 30; italic in the original), we must call into question the fact/value dichotomy.

To be sure, this historical argument is not sufficient in itself to support Putnam's thesis that facts and values are inextricably entangled. At best, it suggests that the fact/value dichotomy is the product of a particular set of philosophical commitments rather than a brute datum with which philosophy must begin. Hence Putnam offers a separate, philosophical argument.

Putnam's philosophical argument for the entanglement thesis begins by calling attention to terms which seem to have both *descriptive* and *prescriptive* elements, what Putnam calls 'thick ethical concepts' (2002: 34). Putnam's example is the term *cruel*. Putman contends that to say of some particular person that he is *cruel* is to morally criticize him. Accordingly, the statement, *He is a very cruel person but nonetheless a good man* strikes us as odd or confused (Putnam 2002: 34). To say of someone that he is cruel is to say that he is *not* overall a good man. This much is obvious. But Putnam contends that *cruel* can be used 'purely descriptively' as well, 'as when a historian writes that a certain monarch was exceptionally cruel, or that the cruelties of the regime provoked a number of rebellions' (2002: 34–5). He concludes that the term *cruel* 'simply ignores that supposed fact/value dichotomy and cheerfully allows itself to be used sometimes for a normative purpose and sometimes as a descriptive term' (2002: 35). Putnam cites other terms that have this tendency, including *brave, temperate, just, rude, generous*, and *elegant*. To *describe* a person or an act with any of these words is at the same time to *evaluate* that person or act. To say of a man that he is *brave* is *both* to describe his actions *and* to morally approve of them. Putnam claims that the existence of such 'thick' concepts undermines the fact/value dichotomy.

Should We Accept the Entanglement Thesis?

The kind of analysis offered by Putnam of the allegedly 'thick' ethical concepts has been the subject of great controversy in contemporary ethical theory. We cannot review these matters here. One question we must ask, however, is whether the fact that certain terms do double-duty as both prescriptive and descriptive entails anything about the fact/value dichotomy.

An obvious response to Putnam's philosophical argument is that the supposedly 'thick' concepts do *not* suggest an entanglement of fact and value, but show only that terms can contain distinctly descriptive and prescriptive elements. Anticipating this response, Putnam argues,

> The attempt . . . to split thick ethical concepts into a 'descriptive meaning component' and a 'prescriptive meaning component' founders on the impossibility of saying what the 'descriptive meaning' of, say, 'cruel' is without using the word 'cruel' or a synonym. (2002: 38)

Putnam's claim that it is *impossible* to make distinct the descriptive element of the term *cruel* seems to beg the question. In response to R. M. Hare's suggestion that the descriptive meaning of *cruel* is captured by 'causing to suffer deeply' (Hare 1981: 74), Putnam contends that 'it is simply not the case' that *cruel* means simply 'causes deep suffering' (2002: 38). But Putnam provides no argument for this. Instead, he presses the point that *suffering* is itself an evaluative, and not simply a descriptive, term. According to Putnam, *suffering* does not just mean *pain*, for, as Putnam points out, it is easy to think of cases of *pain* that are not cases of *suffering*. Similarly, Putnam claims that it is easy to think of cases of someone causing great pain to another which are not cases of *cruelty*; for example, dentists working before the introduction of anesthesia surely caused great pain to their patients, but were not *eo ipso* cruel (2002: 38).

But something has gone awry here. Hare's claim is that the descriptive component of *cruel* can be characterized as *causing to suffer deeply*. However, Putnam's argument attacks the claim that the descriptive component of *cruelty* is captured by *causes great pain*. Yet Hare proposed that *cruelty*, taken descriptively, means *causes great suffering*. Hare did not assert that *suffering*, taken descriptively, means *pain*. So where's the argument?

Perhaps Putnam will want to argue that since *suffering* is not a purely descriptive term (it is itself a 'thick ethical concept'), Hare's analysis of *cruel* in terms of *suffering* fails to capture the *descriptive* component of the term. Why should this be? Why couldn't Hare concede that *suffering* also has a descriptive and a prescriptive component, and that the descriptive meaning of *cruel* can be captured by the descriptive meaning of *suffering*? Putnam is likely to welcome this move, for he has claimed that Hare must mean by *suffering* something descriptive like *pain*. As we saw above, if Hare were to offer *pain* as the descriptive meaning of *suffering*, then Putnam's argument would succeed. But there's no reason to think that the descriptive component of *suffering* is captured by *pain*. As Putnam correctly emphasizes, not all cases of pain are cases of suffering. Hare certainly could concede as much, and then propose that the descriptive content of *suffering* could be captured by a more detailed concept, like *ongoing gratuitous pain*.

Against this analysis of the descriptive component of *suffering*, Putnam might argue, roughly as above, that the term *gratuitous* is not purely descriptive. However, Hare could respond, roughly as above, that *gratuitous* has both a prescriptive and descriptive meaning, and that the descriptive meaning of *suffering* is captured (in part) by the descriptive meaning of *gratuitous*. And so the argument would continue. It is important to note, however, that given the further moves available to the proponent of a position like Hare's, it is far from clear that Putnam is correct to say that, in the case of so-called thick ethical concepts, it is *impossible* to separate out a descriptive meaning and a prescriptive meaning. If Putnam's philosophical argument against the fact/value dichotomy was supposed to demonstrate this impossibility, it does not succeed.

One wonders whether Putnam might see the historical argument as doing the real work against the fact/value dichotomy. Recall that Putnam holds that Quine's arguments in 'Two Dogmas of Empiricism' show that no straightforward dichotomy the analytic and synthetic, or between the *conceptual* (true in virtue of meaning) and the *empirical* (true in virtue of the facts) was possible. As we mentioned, Putnam thinks that both the analytic/synthetic and the fact/value dichotomies employ the very same conception of a *fact*, and it is this conception that is undermined by Quine. It seems natural, then, that Putnam should claim that it is *impossible* to separate out a 'descriptive meaning' and a 'prescriptive meaning' in thick ethical concepts: If Quine is correct, there are no raw or brute facts and thus no distinctively descriptive meaning. That is, if Quine is correct, all meaning involves prescription; accordingly, if Quine is correct, then Putnam is right to say that it is *impossible* to discern a purely descriptive meaning of a term.

It makes sense, then, that Putnam should endorse so fully Quine's attack on the analytic/synthetic dichotomy. Indeed, Putnam goes so far as to claim that Quine's arguments 'demolished the . . . notion of the "analytic" to the satisfaction of most philosophers' (2002: 29). Unfortunately for Putnam, this is an overstatement. The soundness, and even relevance, of Quine's arguments in 'Two Dogmas of Empiricism' has been a matter of dispute ever since Quine published that essay, and it is hardly clear that Quine's position on the matter is the dominant view today. We cannot here address the debates surrounding Quine's position. But it is worth noting that, if we take the historical argument to be Putnam's primary argument against the fact/value dichotomy, then his position seems to amount to this: *If* one accepts Quine's criticism of the analytic/synthetic dichotomy then one should reject the fact/value dichotomy. But this is simply to defend one controversial pragmatist thesis by appeal to another, perhaps even more controversial, pragmatist thesis. It is not clear that we have made any progress in understanding Dewey's and Putnam's proposal that moral inquiry is a species of scientific inquiry.

REFLECTIVE EQUILIBRIUM

The pragmatist proposals we have examined thus far seem to have been agreed on at least one issue: pragmatists must be able to tell a convincing philosophical story about how the questions and concerns typically addressed by ethicists could be fit into a broadly naturalistic view of the world. As we have seen, James sought to tell a story according to which moral statements could be analyzed in terms of psychological states, whereas Dewey and Putnam sought to tell a story according to which the very thought that values need to be *fit* into the natural world is a muddle. We have seen that both proposals face considerable difficulties. We close this chapter with a brief discussion of a different kind of strategy available to pragmatists, what is called the method of *reflective equilibrium*. You will recall the brief discussion of the idea of reflective equilibrium from Chapter 2. Here, we will first describe this method as it applies to moral theory.

Then we will say something about why it is an option that pragmatists should welcome. Finally, we will raise some questions about reflective equilibrium as a method of moral theorizing.

The Idea of Reflective Equilibrium

The idea for a philosophical methodology rooted in reflective equilibrium originates in Nelson Goodman's (1974/1955) work at the intersection of the philosophy of language and the philosophy of science. Goodman was interested in the question of how the logical rules of deduction could be justified. This is a genuine puzzle, since it looks like any proposed justification would have to employ, and thus implicitly presume the correctness of, certain rules of deduction; such a justification would clearly be question-begging. Very roughly, Goodman proposed that the only way to justify our most basic rules of logic is by checking them against the kinds of inferences we intuitively think should be endorsed. Goodman argues,

> Principles of deductive inference are justified by their conformity with accepted deductive practice. Their validity depends upon accordance with the particular deductive inferences we actually make and sanction. If a rule yields inacceptable [sic] inferences, we drop it as invalid. Justification of general rules thus derives from judgments rejecting or accepting particular deductive inferences. (1974/1955: 63)

But note that we justify particular inferences by appeal to general rules of deduction! That is, we say that a particular inference is deductively valid just in case it is an instantiation of a valid pattern of inference, a pattern that employs valid inference rules. As Goodman admits, 'This looks flagrantly circular' (1979: 64).

Goodman contends that the circularity involved in the justification of rules of deductive inference is 'virtuous' rather than vicious (1979: 64). The virtuousness consists in the fact that the process of justification works in both directions: 'A rule is amended if it yields an inference we are unwilling to accept; an inference is rejected if it violates a rule we are unwilling to amend' (1974: 64). The process of justifying rules of inference, then, is on Goodman's analysis the 'delicate' matter of 'making mutual adjustments between rules and accepted inferences' (1974: 64). He adds that 'the agreement achieved' between rules and accepted inferences is 'the only justification needed for either' (1974: 64).

As a methodology for moral theory, reflective equilibrium involves the attempt to judge our moral theories against our considered moral judgments, what are sometimes called our moral *intuitions*.[1] For example, we feel confident that torture is a serious moral wrong; in fact, we feel so confident in this moral judgment that we tend to think that any moral theory that could not support this judgment about torture is *ipso facto* deficient. That is, there are certain intuitive moral judgments that we feel so certain of that we evaluate moral theories in terms of their ability to respect them. Accordingly, it counts *against* a proposed moral theory that it does not prohibit torture. At the same time, however, the reason we engage in moral theorizing *at all* is that we want guidance in making moral judgments. A moral *theory* provides a basis for deciding *what to do* in certain circumstances; that is, we appeal to moral theories to evaluate actions. Hence we see that reflective equilibrium involves a process by which our moral theories and our moral intuitions are tested against one another, with a view to eventually arriving at a moral theory that both squares with our considered moral judgments and provides guidance in cases in which we're not sure what to do.

Of course, reflective equilibrium, once achieved, is not necessarily a stable condition. A given moral theory might square quite well with a wide range of moral intuitions, and thus seem satisfactory, but then yield a counterintuitive result when confronted with new or unusual conditions. In such a case, we need to decide whether to tweak our theory so that it can yield a more plausible result, or accept the counterintuitive result, thereby revising our considered judgment.

Although the process of reflective equilibrium might sound alien, it is in fact quite natural. Notice that we employed this method in our discussion of James's meliorism. Our argument against James was that his moral theory could not condemn certain instances of theft and dishonesty. In making that argument, we were appealing to the moral intuition that stealing is wrong, even if one steals from someone who won't miss what is stolen. Moreover, we were counting on our readers sharing our sense that the fact that James's meliorism cannot accommodate this intuitive judgment should count *against* James's theory. To be sure, a Jamesian could respond that our moral intuitions concerning theft need revision rather than James's moral theory.

In this case, we would raise another kind of case in which it seems that the Jamesian must endorse a counterintuitive result. The challenge to the Jamesian would then be to decide whether to preserve the theory by rejecting the intuition or revise the theory so that it can accommodate the intuition. And so the process goes.

Pragmatism and Reflective Equilibrium

There are several features of the reflective equilibrium model of moral theory that should resonate positively with pragmatists. First, the model of reflective equilibrium requires an *ongoing* engagement between moral theory and moral practice, thereby preserving the pragmatist commitment to the idea that theories must be judged by their implications for practice. Furthermore, the model embraces the kind of fallibilism familiar to pragmatists; on the reflective equilibrium model, both our moral judgments and our moral theories stand in need of revision in light of new circumstances. We should also note that, since the model of reflective equilibrium is concerned to square moral theories against intuitive moral judgments, it requires us to consult with others about how their favored moral theories square with their intuitions, accordingly, appreciate the pragmatist commitment to understanding all inquiry as fundamentally *social*.

Perhaps most importantly, the model of reflective equilibrium aspires to be *noncommittal* on the complicated questions that both the meliorist and the methodist attempt to answer. That is, reflective equilibrium presupposes no particular view of the meaning of moral terms, or of the status of the fact/value distinction. It attempts to proceed with moral theory *without* having to address such matters. Of course, since the method involves the refinement of our moral theories, eventually questions concerning the fact/value distinction and the like will have to be addressed. But the model of reflective equilibrium *denies* that these matters must be dealt with *first*. In this way, the model of reflective equilibrium embodies a kind of *antifoundationalism* about moral justification; unlike other approaches to moral theory which contend that one must give an account of the meaning of moral language *before* one can develop a moral theory and make moral judgments, the model of reflective equilibrium attempts to do everything at once, adjusting our theories and our judgments as we go along.

Problems with Reflective Equilibrium

But there are problems that any advocate of the method of reflective equilibrium must confront. Here we raise only the most obvious kind of difficulty. One might worry that by *beginning* with our intuitive moral judgments, we thereby *privilege* them. Thus it might seem that the method of reflective equilibrium is inherently *conservative*. To be sure, we don't mean here by *conservative* the political platform associated with the Republican Party in the United States; rather, we mean to point out that the model of reflective equilibrium is premised on what we might call a *minimal mutilation principle*. That is, the method of reflective equilibrium begins from the presumption that our considered moral judgments are *roughly* correct and thus should be preserved. Accordingly, any proposed moral theory that would require a *drastic* or *radical* revision of our considered moral judgments would be rejected by the method.

What warrants this? Why should moral theorizing begin from the presumption that whatever seems most morally obvious to us should be treated as *prima facie* correct? It is worth noting that many of the most important moral triumphs we could name – the civil rights movement in the United States, for example – involved a quite drastic revision of moral principles that were at the time taken to be very certainly correct. As it turned out, those considered moral judgments were false. We arguably confront a technological world that poses for us moral problems that are quite unlike the problems our standard moral theories were designed to address. It is likely that our moral intuitions are products of cultural and social conditions that no longer obtain. It could very well be the case that our considered moral judgments are *unfit* to deal with moral questions concerning globalization, the degradation of the environment, the depletion of natural resources, and large-scale economic inequality among people of different nations. Indeed, we will examine some pragmatist responses to questions of environmental ethics in Chapter 7. For now, let us look at some pragmatist view of politics.

CHAPTER 6

PRAGMATISM AND POLITICS

We have examined a variety of pragmatist views concerning knowledge, truth, metaphysics, and ethics. One thought running through these is that philosophy is irreducibly *social*. It should come as no surprise, then, that pragmatism is frequently taken to entail a distinctive political philosophy. In this chapter, we will survey and raise difficulties for four different pragmatist proposals for political philosophy. We begin with Dewey's view that pragmatism entails that 'democracy is a way of life'. Then we turn to Richard Rorty's more modest view that democracy is simply *our* way of life. Next we will examine the minimalist conception of democracy that Richard Posner sees as the upshot of his 'everyday pragmatism'. Finally, we will critically engage Cheryl Misak's epistemic conception of democracy.

DEMOCRACY AS A WAY OF LIFE

What Is Deweyan Democracy?

Of the original pragmatists, only Dewey attended to politics in a systematic way. The core of his political philosophy is his conception of democracy as a 'way of life'. What kind of 'way of life' is democracy? We can begin to understand Deweyan democracy by means of the following characterization: Deweyan democracy is *substantive* rather than thin, *communicative* rather than aggregative, and *deep* rather than statist.[1]

To explain: Deweyan democracy is *substantive* insofar as it rejects any attempt to separate politics and ethics. Dewey held that the democratic political order is essentially a *moral* order, and, further, democratic participation is an essential constituent of a 'truly human way of living' (LW11: 218). Of course, there are different views of democratic participation, and Dewey rejects the idea that participation consists simply in voting and petitioning in service of one's preferences. Thus Dewey held that democratic participation is essentially *communicative*, it consists in the willingness of citizens to engage in activity by which they may 'convince and be convinced by reason' (MW10: 404) and come to realize 'values prized in common' (LW13: 71).[2] Dewey thought that such communicative processes were fit to govern not simply the government, but the whole of social association. Hence democracy is a 'way of life' (LW13: 155) rather than a kind of state (LW2: 325); it is a mode of social organization that 'must affect all modes of human association, the family, the school, industry, religion' (LW2: 325). In this way, Deweyan democracy is *deep*. It reaches into the whole of our lives, both individual and collective, and provides a social ideal of human flourishing, what Dewey called 'growth' (MW12: 181).

Deweyan democracy is a species of *perfectionism*. Perfectionists hold that it is the job of the state to promote or cultivate among citizens the dispositions, habits, and virtues requisite to human flourishing. The perfectionist is to be contrasted with the *neutralist*, who holds that, since people disagree about what human flourishing or the good life consists in, the state must be *impartial* with regard to such matters. According to the neutralist, politics is concerned strictly with the protecting rights of individuals to life, liberty, and property, not their moral development, happiness, or flourishing.

As Dewey sees the self as inherently social, and the good as a matter of self-realization, he held that 'Democracy and the one, ultimate, ethical ideal of humanity are . . . synonyms' (EW1: 248).[3] However, unlike other forms of perfectionism, which hold that the project of forming citizens' dispositions is a task only for the state, Dewey's perfectionism is, like his conception of democracy, *deep*; that is, on the Deweyan view, the perfectionist project is a task for *all* modes of human association (LW2: 325). Dewey held that 'The struggle for democracy has to be maintained on as many fronts as culture has aspects: political, economic, international, educational, scientific and artistic, and religious' (LW13: 186). He saw the task of democracy to be that of 'making our own politics, industry, education, our culture generally, a servant and an evolving manifestation of democratic ideals' (LW13: 197). For Dewey, then, *all* social associations should be aimed at the realization of his distinctive vision of human flourishing.

This aspiration is found throughout Dewey's corpus; in his writings on politics, education, psychology, religion, culture, and art, we are told that growth is the ultimate and proper end.

The Problem of Pluralism

Perfectionism faces a serious difficulty. Perfectionists hold that the state must endeavor to promote some specified moral end, such as growth; consequently, perfectionism is rooted in the judgment that we *know* what it is for humans to flourish, and thus that further philosophical disputation over the question of human flourishing is superfluous. This is especially evident in Dewey's case, for Dewey proposes to structure *all of society* around his own view of human flourishing. One must have a markedly high level of confidence in the correctness of one's conception of human flourishing if one is to prescribe it *for everyone*.

Do we know what it is for humans to flourish? This question is not skeptical or nihilistic. We are not raising the possibility that such knowledge is impossible; nor are we suggesting that the very idea is nonsensical. Rather, we are raising the concern that, given the state of our moral knowledge, no one yet *knows* which conception of human flourishing is correct. Indeed, when we survey the fields of philosophy, economics, theology, psychology, sociology, and biology, we find *several* competing conceptions of human flourishing. Similarly, when we canvass our fellow citizens, we discover a plurality of conceptions of what is best in life, what is most important, and what it means to live well. What's more, we find that, for the most part, each of these varied visions of human flourishing has its distinctive strengths and weaknesses; there are several competing conceptions of human flourishing that are philosophically viable and it is hard to declare any clear winner among them.

Hence the difficulty: Before we propose to organize society around any conception of human flourishing in particular, we had better be sure we have the right or best one, for it is clear that a state which imposes on its citizens a *false* or *defective* conception of human flourishing inflicts serious moral harms on them. The difficulty is especially pressing in the case of Deweyan democracy, which envisions a society in which *all* modes of human association are aimed toward the promotion of Dewey's conception of flourishing.

Of course, the Deweyan contends that since he has the *correct* conception of human flourishing, he needn't worry about this difficulty. But how can he be so sure? Is his confidence warranted? One way for the Deweyan to justify his confidence is for him to supply the reasons which support his conception of human flourishing. The Deweyan thus offers a detailed account beginning with Dewey's Darwininan conception of the human organism and his corresponding experimentalist conception of experience, and culminating in Dewey's theory of inquiry, which in turn underwrites his conception of growth. But simply supplying the philosophical back story to growth does not assuage the difficulty. The Deweyan must also show how his own view is *superior* to its competitors. Here is where the real difficulty lies. Many of the competing views of human flourishing can supply similarly detailed philosophical accounts of themselves; they, too, can articulate a compelling philosophical system which underwrites their moral philosophy. As the thousands of books and articles that are published yearly on these topics show, the question of which conception of human flourishing at best is yet an open question. Hence the Deweyan cannot claim to have the final word. The project of instituting 'democracy as a way of life' by designing all institutions of human association so that they promote growth is at best premature.

The fact that the Deweyan democratic program is premature might not deter the Deweyan. She might concede that there is sufficient disagreement among philosophers, theologians, economists, psychologists, and persons on the street to constitute a serious obstacle to the practical project of reconstructing our social world so that it becomes 'a servant and an evolving manifestation of democratic ideals' (LW13: 197). But she could maintain that extensive disagreement does not disprove the Deweyan conception of human flourishing. The Deweyan could maintain that she has offered an *ideal* for a democratic society, a picture of what it would mean for democracy to be realized fully, not a blueprint or algorithm for remaking society.

Now we must ask whether Deweyan democracy is appropriate even as an *ideal* for a democratic society to strive for. The work of John Rawls supplies a compelling argument *against* Deweyan democracy as an ideal. Rawls contends that any free society is marked by what he calls 'the fact of reasonable pluralism' (1996: 36). We have encountered the term *pluralism* in our previous discussions of metaphysics and ethics; in the present context, the term means something slightly different from both.[4] Basically, Rawls's claim is this: There is no single conception of human flourishing upon which reason converges. However, there is a set of defensible and reasonable conceptions of human flourishing (what Rawls calls 'comprehensive doctrines') such that each is fully consistent with the best exercise of reason but inconsistent with other members of the set. Consequently, Rawls holds that despite 'our conscious attempt to reason with each other' (1996: 55), agreement at the level of our comprehensive doctrines is elusive. Importantly, Rawls contends that reasonable pluralism 'is not a mere historical condition that may soon pass away' (1996: 36), but 'the long-run outcome of the work of human reason under enduring free institutions' (1996: 129). That is, the very liberties secured in a democracy give rise to reasonable pluralism.

The flip-side of the fact of reasonable pluralism is what Rawls calls the 'fact of oppression' (1996: 36). If reasonable pluralism is 'the inevitable outcome of free human reason', then 'a continuing shared understanding on one comprehensive doctrine can be maintained only by the oppressive use of state power' (1996: 36). In other words, Rawls contends that where minds are free, pluralism prevails; where pluralism does not prevail, minds are not free.

The outcome of Rawls's view about reasonable pluralism is that 'no comprehensive doctrine is appropriate as a political conception for a constitutional regime' (1996: 135); that is, no theory of human flourishing, no matter how philosophically well developed, could serve as the ideal for a modern democracy. For in such a democracy, there will necessarily be a reasonable pluralism of theories of human flourishing, and to construct a society according to one of these reasonable views is to oppress those who subscribe to any of its reasonable competitors. Consequently, a 'well-ordered democratic society' cannot be a community, if by 'community' we mean 'a special kind of association, one united by a comprehensive doctrine' (1996: 40). But a community is precisely what the Deweyan thinks democracy should aspire to. Deweyan democracy must reject the fact of reasonable pluralism; it is thus oppressive in Rawls's sense.

A Response and Further Difficulties

In response, the Deweyan will question the Rawlsian conception of reasonable pluralism. Couldn't the claim that it is a fact be rejected? The answer is no. To see why, first let us make more explicit what the fact of reasonable pluralism is. Reflect for a moment upon current political and moral circumstances. Although much of the strife and conflict in our society is arguably due to various forms of irrationality – greed, ignorance, hatred, envy, what have you – a large measure of disagreement and discord occurs among persons who are not only able to articulate good reasons and arguments for their positions, but also willing and able to engage sincerely and respectfully with those with whom they disagree. Hence it is not difficult to find a wide variety of distinct and well-reasoned positions on every major moral and social question. Now, of course, each of us must take it that those who hold moral positions and doctrines that are inconsistent with our own are *mistaken*; but an intellectually honest engagement with our most sophisticated opponents leads us to recognize that there is a crucial difference between being *wrong* and being *stupid*. We may say, then, that, the fact of reasonable pluralism is simply the fact that in a free society it is easy to find intelligent and reasoned opposition to every moral, philosophical, or religious doctrine. Accordingly, to *reject* the fact of reasonable pluralism is to reject the distinction between being wrong and being stupid; it is to say that anyone who does not agree with your own particular view of things is not simply *mistaken* but *benighted, ignorant*, or *foolish*. To reject the fact of reasonable pluralism is to be a dogmatist, or perhaps a *fanatic*. Accordingly, it is difficult to see how one could reject the fact of reasonable pluralism. More importantly, given that Deweyan pragmatism is a species of fallibilism, no Deweyan could reject the fact of reasonable pluralism.

A closely related point is crucial. As we have said, the fact of reasonable pluralism is simply the fact that reasonable, sincere persons doing their epistemic best and attending carefully to all the relevant considerations can nevertheless disagree fundamentally about moral, religious, and philosophical essentials. Accordingly, even if one concedes the *correctness* of the entirety of Deweyan pragmatism, the criticism we have raised of Deweyan democracy stands. This is because the objection is not that the philosophical commitments that constitute Deweyan democracy are *false*, but only that they are *reasonably rejectable*; those who reject Deweyan democracy might be *ipso facto* mistaken, but they are *not* therefore *unreasonable* or *unfit* for democratic citizenship. Put otherwise, a comprehensive doctrine must satisfy a standard higher than truth (or correctness) if it is to be an appropriate basis for public policy and decision; that standard is that the doctrine must not be reasonably rejectable. The fact of reasonable pluralism entails that no comprehensive doctrine meets this standard.

Hence it will not do for Deweyans to respond to the objection we have raised by offering philosophical arguments for their core commitments. No amount of philosophical maneuvering will do, because the truth of Deweyan pragmatism is not at issue; in fact, it may be granted for the purposes of this argument. Barring the untenable response that all non-Deweyans are *ipso facto* stupid or ignorant, the only recourse open to the Deweyan democrat is to recognize that her conception of democracy, along with its constituent vision of human flourishing, is but one reasonable comprehensive doctrine among many. This realization will lead the Dewey to *privatize* her project, to see Deweyan democracy as a 'way of life' in a *personal* sense, and not something fit to be woven into the very fabric of our entire society.

But to privatize in this way would be to *abandon* Deweyan democracy to a very significant extent. Crucially, a *privatized* Deweyan would have to renounce Dewey's philosophy of public education, since it advocates the reconstruction of public schools so that they contribute to the realization of Dewey's comprehensive doctrine. More generally, a privatized Deweyan would have to abandon the idea that democracy presents the 'task before us' (LW14: 224) of creating a way of social life marked by the 'possession and continual use of certain attitudes, forming personal character and determining desire and purpose in all the relations of life' (LW14: 225–6). Similarly, a privatized Deweyan would have to reject Dewey's claim that democracy is 'radical' because it requires 'great change in existing social institutions, economic, legal and cultural' (LW11: 299). That is to say, a privatized Deweyan democrat is arguably not a Deweyan democrat at all.

Hence the privatization strategy does not seem available to the Deweyan. What's a Deweyan democrat to do? It seems she must either reject fact of reasonable pluralism or show how Deweyan democracy is consistent with the fact of reasonable pluralism. Rejecting the fact of reasonable pluralism seems problematic, especially for a Deweyan: that reasonable people disagree sharply over comprehensive doctrines is a markedly evident aspect of modern life. So the first horn is not promising. As for the second horn, in order to render Deweyan democracy consistent with reasonable pluralism, the Deweyan will have to relinquish much of the perfectionism of Deweyan democracy. But once the perfectionism is surrendered, it is difficult to know what to make of the claim that democracy is a 'way of life'. The thought that democracy is not a kind of state but a way of life seems to be the fulcrum of Deweyan democracy.

DEMOCRACY AS OUR WAY OF LIFE

The Aim of Political Philosophy

It should be noted that our discussion of Deweyan democracy above presupposed a particular view of what political philosophy is. Specifically, we presumed that the political philosopher is in the business of developing and articulating arguments that support conclusions concerning how we ought to live together. Richard Rorty has proposed a different view of the task of political philosophy. According to Rorty, political philosophers ought to seek to inspire 'social hope' (1999) and 'national pride' (1998); that is, according to Rorty, political theorists should tell 'inspiring stories' (1998: 3) that '[clear] philosophy out of the way' and 'let the imagination play upon the possibilities of a utopian future' (1999: 239). Rorty holds that it is through inspiration, not argumentation – through appreciation of the lives of Walt Whitman and John Dewey (1998: 11) not through engagement with the arguments of political theorists such as Martha Nussbaum or Ronald Dworkin – that democratic citizens will come to see themselves as 'part of a great human adventure' (1999: 239).

Rorty hence abandons the traditional aspirations of political philosophy in the same way he abandons the traditional aspirations of epistemology and metaphysics. Whereas thinkers such as Locke, Kant, Mill, and Rawls sought after philosophical principles that could provide the groundwork for a democratic order, Rorty insists that democracy 'can get along without philosophical presuppositions' (1988: 178), and that 'democracies are now in a position to throw away some of the ladders used in their own construction' (1989: 194). In keeping with the general thrust of his pragmatism, Rorty holds that we should give up the idea that democratic politics is 'subject to the jurisdiction of a philosophical tribunal' (1989: 196–7); he contends that the traditional hunt for a philosophical justification for democracy is merely a 'distraction' (1996: 335).

Distraction from what? What is left for political philosophy to do once we follow Rorty in abandoning the search for the philosophical foundations of democracy? Despite his varied claims to be involved in a 'post-philosophical' project, Rorty's politics is couched in a more general philosophical perspective that we may call 'political anti-foundationalism'. Rorty's notion of an antifoundationalist political philosophy is best understood in contrast with his understanding of what it means to be a democratic foundationalist, so it is with this contrast that we begin.[5]

Democracy without Foundations

Rorty characterizes the democratic foundationalist as holding that 'political institutions are no better than their philosophical foundations' (1988: 178); the foundationalist therefore seeks a philosophical *proof* of democracy. That is, in similar fashion to foundationalists in epistemology, the democratic foundationalist wants an argument that establishes the justice and superiority of democracy from self-evident or otherwise unavoidable premises. As these premises must be such as to win the assent of antidemocrats,[6] they must not beg the question in the democrat's favor and therefore must appeal to something beyond existing democratic practices. That is, the case for democracy must begin from some fact or principle that is *external* to democracy; according to Rorty, foundationalists typically appeal to supposed facts about 'human nature', 'rationality', or 'morality' for the needed premises (1996: 333).

Foundationalists thus try to establish the justice of democracy by 'driving' antidemocrats 'against an argumentative wall' of unavoidable first principles (1989: 53). The foundationalist suspects that democracy is 'enfeebled' unless it can be shown to follow from such principles (1996: 335). The job of the foundationalist philosopher of democracy, therefore, is to *refute* antidemocrats by showing that the proposition 'democracy is the best form of government' (or some such proposition) follows from a set of principles that they implicitly accept.

Rorty insists that the traditional attempt to 'ground' democracy is futile because it is couched in an obsolete and naïve philosophical paradigm. According to Rorty,

> There is no way to beat [e.g.,] totalitarians in argument by appealing to shared common premises, and no point in pretending that [e.g.,] a common human nature makes the totalitarians unconsciously hold such premises. (1987: 42)

Moreover, Rorty contends that 'attempts to ground a practice on something outside the practice will always be more or less disingenuous' (1996: 333). He holds that the lesson we must learn from the failure of the Enlightenment is that 'human beings are historical all the way through' (1988: 176), that there are no external facts about 'human nature', 'rationality', or 'morality' that supply a foundational premise. Accordingly, he claims that any proposed foundation for democracy will inevitably be 'just a hypostatization of certain selected components' of existing democratic practice (1996: 333–4). Rorty explains:

> To say that a certain course of conduct is more in accord with human nature or our moral sense, or more rational, than another is just a fancy way of commending one's own sense of what is most worth preserving in our present practices, of commending our own utopian vision of our community. (1996: 334)

According to Rorty, then, we must abandon the foundationalist aspiration for a philosophical proof of democracy and embrace the thoroughgoing contingency of our language, our selves, and our society (1989); we must give up the idea that democrats need to refute antidemocrats.[7] On the antifoundationalist view, political philosophy is not the search for foundations, but simply a contest between different 'idealizations' of existing social practices. An idealization of a social practice is a vision of 'the utopian future of our community' which 'suck[s] up and concentrate[s] intuitions about the importance of certain components of our practices' (1996: 333). Hence, Rorty describes the difference between John Rawls's defense of the welfare state and Robert Nozick's libertarian view as the 'competition between the two men's idealizations' of 'present practices in the liberal democracies'. On Rorty's reading, 'Rawls's principles remind us of what we do in our appellate courts, whereas Nozick's remind us of what we do in our marketplaces'. The difference between the welfare state and the minimal state, then, is simply 'a matter of playing certain of our practices against others' (1996: 333). That is, according to Rorty, there is really nothing like a *philosophical* dispute going on between those who, like Rawls, support a scheme of progressive taxation because they hold that 'social and economic inequalities are to be arranged so that they are . . . to the greatest benefit of the least advantaged' (Rawls 1999: 266) and those who, like Nozick, contend that taxation is 'on a par with forced labor' (Nozick 1974: 169); on Rorty's view, there is no dispute between these views, but only a *contest* among different prioritizations of our intuitions and practices.

Having given up on the idea of a philosophical proof of democracy, the antifoundationalist offers a 'circular justification' for his idealization; he 'makes one feature of our culture look good by citing still another', and unabashedly compares our culture with others 'by reference to our own standards' (1989: 57). By promoting a particular idealization of his community, the antifoundationalist does not provide a foundation (albeit a relativist one) for the practices he idealizes, and he is not supplying 'philosophical backup' for those aspects of his community that he most admires. Rather, he is 'putting politics first and tailoring a philosophy to suit' (1988: 178).

Hence Rorty claims that our conception of democracy is simply our conception of *our* way of life. What may look like different conceptions of democracy or opposed political philosophies are simply different descriptions of how we and others like us get along. By offering a philosophical articulation of democracy, one does not offer anything like an *argument* or a *justification* for democracy; one simply proffers an 'idealization' of democracy. Rorty does not lament this, however. He insists that the purposes of democracy are *better served* by the antifoundationalist strategy. Rorty claims that 'The search for foundations of democracy' is a 'distraction from debates between competing idealizations of current practices' (1996: 335).

In Rorty's ideal 'post philosophical' and 'poeticized' (1989: 53) culture of 'postmodernist bourgeois liberalism' (1983), citizens would openly acknowledge the contingency of their liberal democratic commitments, yet nonetheless 'stand unflinchingly' (1989: 46) for them. This 'unflinching courage' (1989: 47) in the face of radical contingency is the essence of what Rorty calls 'liberal ironism'.

Criticizing Rorty

Rorty's many critics have charged that his ironic liberalism is relativist, irrationalist, emotivist, ethnocentric, self-defeating, and nonprogressive. However, Rorty is not bothered by such criticisms; in response, he simply insists that such charges will offend only those who are still practicing the kind of philosophy he has abandoned. For example, to the charge that his antifoundationalism is irrationalist and emotivist, Rorty responds that only those who accept an archaic moral psychology – namely, one that 'distinguishes between reason and the passions' – could make such a charge (1996: 334). Similarly, to the suggestion that his account is ethnocentric, Rorty responds that it is because 'the philosophical tradition has accustomed us to the idea that anybody who is willing to listen to reason – to hear out all arguments – can be brought around to the truth' that one worries about 'ethnocentrism' in political philosophy (1988: 188). Rorty rejects these philosophical fantasies, and any criticism that tacitly employs such principles may be dismissed as question-begging.

A different strategy is thus required. Since we cannot engage Rorty on the familiar territory of philosophy, where circularity, ethnocentrism, and self-defeatingness are to be avoided, we must press Rorty on other grounds. Specifically, we would like to examine Rorty's contention that that democracy is better served by his anti-foundationalist and ironic politics.

Let us then suppose that Rorty's ironic vision of a liberal democratic utopia has been widely accepted. We thus imagine that the political theorists of the world no longer write pieces with foreboding and serious titles like *The Foundations of Liberal Equality* and *Justice as Impartiality*; they hence no longer see their philosophical opponents as misguided and mistaken, but simply enchanted by different political visions that inspire different idealizations of political practice. The contest between these different idealizations is no longer understood as a search for the True or the Right, but as something like a political campaign: each political theorist *promotes* his idealization and tries to inspire his fellow citizens. We hold that Rorty's liberal ironism is in many respects undesirable. Most generally, we contend that Rorty's view is unable to respond convincingly to contemporary political realities and hence unable to inspire the kind of social hope and solidarity he aims to invoke.

Idealizations and Political Realities

We begin with a basic point about Rorty's reduction of political controversies to contests among idealizations. This makes sense *only if* we restrict our analyses to congenial disputes between professional academics such as Rawls and Nozick. Rorty's view breaks down when we consider the more fundamental disputes that arise outside the academy. Consider, for example, Stalin's claim that his brutal regime is democratic 'in a higher sense'. Does it make sense to say that Stalinism is just another idealization of democracy? The obvious response, one that Rorty endorses (1998: 57–8), is that Stalinist democracy is not democracy at all. However, it is unclear how Rorty can make the distinction between *real* democracy and tyranny-disguised-as-democracy while remaining faithful to his antifoundationalism. Perhaps Rorty would like to treat Stalin as he would treat Nietzsche and Loyola. That is, perhaps he will avoid having to distinguish real democracy from tyranny by simply dismissing Stalin as *mad*. Of course, for Rorty to call Stalin mad is not to issue a psychological diagnosis, but simply to say that 'there is no way to see [him] as [a] fellow [citizen] of our constitutional democracy'; Rorty thinks Stalin is 'crazy' because 'the limits of sanity are set by what *we* can take seriously' (1988: 187). According to Rorty, these limits are, of course, 'determined by our upbringing, our historical situation' (1988: 188). Once again we see that, for Rorty, democratic theory is simply the articulation of *our* way of life.

This admittedly 'ethnocentric' (1988: 188) strategy founders once we consider cases of *fellow citizens* who promote idealizations of our democracy that are similar to those proffered by Stalin, or Hitler, or any of Rorty's other paradigmatic madmen. Members of white-supremacist or other racist organizations certainly promote a certain vision of the 'utopian future of our community' (1996: 333), a particular image of what is best in our culture. We cannot treat racists as 'mad' *and* maintain that 'the limits of sanity' are set by the contingencies of community, for, in this case, the 'madmen' are *members* of my community; the KKK is as much a part of our social inheritance as the ACLU and the AFL-CIO. Rorty must either introduce some ad hoc qualifications to the terms 'idealization' 'ethnocentrism', and 'social practice', such that the racist will necessarily not count as 'one of us', or he will have to concede that the modern democratic state is home to persons who promote views that differ substantially from his own.

Current political realities suggest that we cannot afford to treat philosophical disputes about politics in the way that Rorty recommends; there is much more at stake in some disputes than 'idealizations'. We must face the fact that, in the interests of the kind of open discussion that is requisite to self-government, a democratic regime allows an extremely wide variety of political organizations to operate. Some of these agencies aim to use democratic liberties to undermine democracy.

Although Rorty is surely aware of such threats, his antifounda-tionalism leaves his political theory impotent to respond. He suggests that, when dealing with opponents of democracy, we 'ask [them] to *privatize* their projects' (1989: 197; italic in the original). And what shall we do when they refuse? We simply change the subject or end the conversation; we 'refuse to argue' with them (1988: 190). Against Rorty's strategy of nonengagement, Robert Dahl has urged the following consideration:

> [L]et us imagine a country with democratic political institutions in which intellectual elites are in the main convinced that democracy *cannot* be justified on reasonable and plausible grounds. The pre-vailing view among them, let us suppose, is that no intellectually respectable reasons exist for believing that a democratic system is better than a nondemocratic alternative. As long as the political, social, and economic institutions of the country are performing adequately from the perspective of the general population, per-haps most people will simply ignore the querulous dissent of their intellectuals; and political leaders and influential opinion makers may in the main go along with the generally favorable popular view. But in time of serious crisis – and all countries go through time of serious crisis – those who try to defend democracy will find the going much harder, while those who promote nondemo-cratic alternatives will find it that much easier. (1996: 338; italic in the original)

This kind of reply might appear overtly alarmist and exaggerated; however, we may consider the growing body of social scientific literature that tells the fascinating yet disturbing tale of increasing voter ignorance and nonparticipation, the breakdown of civic asso-ciation, the loss of community, and the reduction of toleration to the 'NIMBY' phenomenon. Hence we may cast Dahl's remarks in a slightly different light: Rorty's strategy of dismissing democracy's enemies rather than attempting to engage them is likely to *strengthen* the antidemocratic forces that are already operative within our soci-ety, and thus might even help to precipitate the kind of crisis that Dahl describes. Here it is important to note that the antidemocratic forces operative within our society *do* propose philosophical argu-ments in favor of their views, they believe that they have *good reasons* to hold the positions they do. Similarly, politically disengaged and apathetic citizens are not simply 'uninspired', but often believe that they are *justified* in ignoring politics, and they typically maintain that political action and engagement are futile. A philosophy that is resolutely opposed to engaging antidemocrats and apathetic citizens *on their own terms* is unable to address these phenomena and consequently unable to work toward their amelioration.

Can Social Hope Be Ironic?

Insofar as Rorty's antifoundationalist politics is unable to confront social forces operative within our society which disable democracy, Rorty's proposal for a 'post philosophical' and 'ironist' approach to democracy seems unsatisfactory. Rorty may of course dismiss the foregoing argument as yet another bit of the kind of philosophy he has abandoned. Hence we'd like to draw this discussion to a close by raising a criticism of Rorty's idea of social hope.

Rorty's antifoundationalism places liberal democracy on a philosophical par with tyranny. On Rorty's view, there is nothing one can say against tyranny that should count as a good reason for the tyrant to become a democrat. Rorty further contends that giving up the Enlightenment illusion that tyrants can somehow be refuted will improve existing democracies. Once political theorists give up the 'distraction' (1996: 133) of trying to develop foundations for democracy, they can take up their proper work of helping to inspire within democratic citizens the social hope requisite to 'achieving' our country.

The inspired fascination with democracy that Rorty seeks to cultivate *is* important; however, an essential component of hope is the confidence that what is hoped for is in some relevant way *worth* achieving and *better* than the other things that might develop. Yet Rorty's antifoundationalism does not allow one to maintain that democracy is in any relevant sense *better* than, say, tyranny or oligarchy. Hence Rorty's 'social hope' must be 'ironic' – we must hope to achieve that which we no longer can think is *worth* achieving, we must draw inspiration from that which we contend is essentially not really inspiring. The idea of an 'ironic' hope is incoherent, and Rorty's politics is literally *hopeless*.

Let us make the point in another way. If there is anything inspiring in the works of Rorty's democratic heroes, it is precisely the sense that the visions of democracy they present are in a nonironic sense *worth* trying for and *worth* hoping to achieve. This can be maintained only if one can point to some aspect of democracy that relevantly distinguishes it from tyranny. But to undertake the project of distinguishing tyranny from democracy is to engage in the kind of foundationalist political theorizing that Rorty has abandoned.

MINIMALIST DEMOCRACY

Everyday Pragmatism

Thus far, we have argued that the Deweyan view of 'democracy as a way of life' is insufficiently pluralistic to serve as an ideal for a modern democratic society. We then argued that Rorty's ironic antifoundationalism is too philosophically flimsy to support the kind of social hope he wants to inspire. We turn next to the views of Richard Posner. We begin with a word about Posner's 'everyday pragmatism' and then critically examine his positive conception of democracy.[8]

Posner advocates a stance he calls 'everyday pragmatism' (2003: ch. 1), which he characterizes as 'the mindset denoted by the popular usage of the word "pragmatic", meaning practical and business-like, "no-nonsense", disdainful of abstract theory and intellectual pretension, contemptuous of moralizers and utopian dreamers' (2003: 50). Posner continues that this mindset 'has been and remains the untheorized cultural outlook of most Americans' (2003: 50); it is the practice of prioritizing the 'empirical over the theoretical' and the methodological directive to 'start from what we have' (2003: 184). In Posner's view, then, pragmatism is a decidedly *antiphilosophical* stance that rejects the very idea of moral and political *theory*. According to the everyday pragmatist, moral and political questions fall within the purview of either the behavioral sciences, such as economics and psychology, or are simply matters of legislation to be settled by legislators and judges.[9]

Two Concepts of Democracy

Much of recent theorizing about democracy has agreed with Dewey that democracy requires more than voting booths and campaigns. As we say earlier, Dewey held that democracy requires *communication* among citizens and the participation of citizens in the processes of self-government. Many theorists of democracy working today contend that *collective deliberation* is an essential ingredient of democracy; that is, theorists propose that the democratic process must include, prior to voting, episodes of *open and public deliberation* among citizens. In such encounters, citizens are supposed to exchange their reasons for the political opinions they hold; in this way, citizens express *reciprocity*, which is taken by deliberative democrats to be the proper attitude among democratic citizens.[10]

Given his commitment to everyday pragmatism, we should expect Posner to reject deliberative democracy. Indeed, in his book *Law, Pragmatism, and Democracy* (2003) and related essays (2002, 2004), Posner raises several objections to what he calls 'Concept 1' democratic theories, by which he means principally 'the loftier forms of 'deliberative democracy' (2003: 130). In place of such views, Posner proposes 'Concept 2' democracy, according to which democracy is 'a kind of market' (2003: 166), a 'competitive power struggle among members of a political elite . . . for the electoral support of the masses' (2003: 130). We believe that many forms of deliberative democracy can withstand Posner's critique of Concept 1 views; however, we cannot pursue this point here. (In the next section of this chapter we examine closely a pragmatist version of deliberative democratic theory.) Instead we shall launch an immanent criticism of Posner's alternative view. More specifically, we shall argue that Posner's 'everyday pragmatism' is at odds with his Concept 2 view of democracy.

Posner's Concept 2 democratic theory is a standard form of the kind of view known as *democratic realism*. Democratic realism has its source in Joseph Schumpeter's classic book, *Capitalism, Socialism, and Democracy* (1962). In that book, Schumpeter famously defines democracy as 'that institutional arrangement for arriving at political decision in which individuals acquire the power to decide by means of a competitive struggle for the people's vote' (1962: 269). Democratic realists, then, stand in stark opposition to any participatory or deliberative conception of democracy; according to the democratic realist, democracy *simply is* voting. In fact, Schumpeter claims that once a citizen casts his vote, his mission as citizen has been fulfilled; consequently, Schumpeter holds that 'once [citizens] have elected an individual, political action is his business and not theirs' (1962: 295). What may seem like ordinary democratic activities, such as standard forms of petition or contributing to grassroots political organizations, are on Schumpeter's view 'political back-seat driving' and are thus to be discouraged (1962: 295). Accordingly, democratic realism is often called *democratic minimalism*.

Drawing upon Schumpeter's minimalism, Posner professes to eschew the utopianism of deliberative theories (2003: 164) by sticking to what he sees as the humble facts about contemporary democracy: Citizens do not care much about politics, they are not very intelligent, and they 'have no interest in debate' (2004: 42). Posner reasons that democracy is therefore best conceived of as a market of 'consumer sovereignty' (2004: 41) in which the 'natural leaders' compete for the votes of the 'sheep' (2003: 183). Contending that his view is 'more respectful of people as they actually are', he characterizes his position as 'realistic' (2003: 165) and 'unillusioned' (2003: 145).

One might object that democratic minimalism paints a thoroughly unflattering picture of democratic citizens. We agree; however, to say that a theory is unflattering is not to criticize it. In fact, despite its unflattering elements, democratic minimalism is a powerful and popular theory of how democracy works. We cannot here engage in a sustained evaluation of minimalism.[11] However, we can raise a concern about Posner's appeal to minimalism as the upshot of his pragmatism. Specifically, we shall argue that everyday pragmatism and democratic realism are in fact not complementary views. To show this, we shall first argue that the 'untheorized cultural outlook of most Americans' conflicts with the democratic realist's model of political action. Then we shall argue that democratic realism conflicts with everyday pragmatism insofar as it aspires to be a scientific theory of democracy.

Are Everyday Pragmatism and Democratic Realism Compatible?

In order to build his everyday pragmatist case for democratic realism, Posner appeals to a formidable body of data that indicate sharp declines in voter participation and similarly sharp increases in voter ignorance. From the point of view of this data, the everyday pragmatist case for democratic realism seems clear – Americans in fact care little about politics. However, that Posner should consider only the data collected by academic social scientists is puzzling. If we turn to other features of our politics, our sense of 'the untheorized cultural outlook of most Americans' becomes more complicated.

Consider that one of the striking features of current modes of political discourse is that they are couched in a self-image that is thoroughly epistemic.[12] Television news channels profess to offer 'no spin' zones and 'fair and balanced' reporting that is 'accurate' and 'trusted'. Popular books of political commentary and criticism, the publication of which is now a multimillion dollar industry, claim to expose 'lying liars' and various other sources of 'fraud', 'illusion', and 'deception'. Popular critiques of the media target 'bias' and 'propaganda'. On political talk radio programming across the nation, citizens participate daily in political discussion that at times involves significant degrees of complexity.[13] Popular criticism of George W. Bush, both in the United States and abroad, focuses almost exclusively on his intelligence, truthfulness, and judgment. Similarly, representatives and pundits are commonly criticized for being 'partisan', that is, blindly loyal to a prefabricated party line and thus irresponsive to the arguments and reasons offered by the opposition.

For the most part this epistemic self-image is *merely* an image. Perhaps it is a mirage. To be sure, the incessant claims to epistemic fairness, reasonableness, trustworthiness, and honesty function mostly as slogans serving marketing and public relations objectives. However, in light of the market pressures operative in the modern media industry, we must conclude that such slogans are effective – they *sell*. These slogans sell precisely because citizens tend to see themselves as well informed and rational; they tend to see their political opinions as based on reasons and argument rather than expressions of raw preferences. At the very least, they hold that reasons, evidence, argument, and truth *matter* for political discourse and decision.

That is, our public culture of political discourse is quasi-deliberative. The various media outlets promote a unified view of what proper democratic politics should be. Specifically, they promote the view that democratic politics involves a fair and balanced ongoing critical exchange of reasons and arguments among honest, knowledgeable, and earnest political inquirers. Even slight deviations from these norms are quickly criticized, and the norms are reinforced, at least in speech, at every turn. As a characterization of our 'untheorized cultural outlook', democratic realism seems inadequate.

Posner will be unimpressed. He recognizes that 'political rhetoric is deeply hypocritical' and that politicians must 'flatter the people and exaggerate the degree to which the people actually rule' (2003: 153). He will maintain that the character of our public political self-image is, again, beside the point. He will insist that no matter what we may *believe* about ourselves, the fact remains that people are uninterested in political participation of the sort that the deliberative democrat prescribes. But, if Posner is correct here, it is difficult to see why the hypocrisy and rhetoric is *necessary*. To repeat, the deliberative self-image may be merely a rhetorical or strategic device, but its prevalence is a prima facie indicator of its effectiveness, and its effectiveness indicates that the deliberative image resonates positively with citizens. That is, if it were true that citizens see their political activity as being no different from purchasing a toaster (Posner 2004: 41), the rhetoric of deliberation and participation would have no purchase. But clearly it *does* have a purchase.

Of course, these considerations constitute no objection to demo-cratic realism per se. The realist cares not for what people *believe* of themselves or how they *understand* their political activity. However, if the everyday pragmatist's mission is to capture the man-on-the-street view of politics, 'the untheorized cultural outlook of most Americans' (2003: 50), then democratic realism misses the mark.

If the foregoing argument goes through, then we have a good rea-son to think that minimalism is not the view of democracy that the everyday pragmatist is looking for. Yet we can push the criticism a bit further to show that everyday pragmatism is not the philosophical framework most congenial to democratic realism. Recall that Posner enlists democratic realism in his antitheory campaign; he advocates realism as a hard-nosed alternative to abstract and aspirational polit-ical theories. However, no democratic realist can abide Posner's antitheory directives. Standard versions of democratic realism, such as Schumpeter's, are technically robust social scientific *theories* and so are thoroughly academic – they are addressed mainly to social scientists for the purpose of explaining and predicting the political behavior of a given population.[14] Accordingly, such views are decid-edly *not* proposed as a description of 'the untheorized cultural outlook of most Americans'. In fact, as critics frequently note, realist models of democracy are replete with ontological, methodological, and moral commitments that are 'abstract' and 'philosophical' in the senses Posner deplores.[15]

Further, we must not overlook the fact that contemporary citizens will not recognize *themselves* in the democratic realist's theory. Consider that according to Posner's realism, political argument is simply rhe-torical bargaining, political speech is simply demagoguery, political commentary is simply the expression of blind interests, and political action is simply the assertion of preference. One may accept this image as a *third-personal account*, that is, as a depiction of how *others* operate, but when this third-personal account is considered from a first-personal perspective – when it is taken as an account of one's *own* political behavior – it looses its credibility. Posner's view requires that we – all of us – understand our *own* political commitments as expressions of raw preference, not the outcome of sincere attempts to weight various arguments, considerations, and evidence. According to Posner, when you enter into political discussion with your friends, you are simply campaigning for your respective preferences; when you attempt to formulate a rational reply to an objection someone has raised against your position, you are in fact merely *rationalizing*. When you criticize your friend for being uncharitable, dishonest, or unfair to your views, you are being hypocritical. Insofar as you believe that this description of your activities, if true, is problematic and lamentable, you are deluded.

Our point here is not the morally optimistic one that citizens are nobler than Posner's view allows. It is rather that citizens generally understand their political opinions to be more than simple preferences and so they typically see their political activities as something different from their consumer activities. Put more strongly, our everyday practices of popular political discourse indicate that citizens generally take their political beliefs to stand in need of arguments and evidence and they think that political *argument*, as distinct from political *bargaining*, is possible. Consequently, Posner's description misrepresents this common aspect of democratic practice.

Admittedly, this does not in itself constitute an objection. However, note that on Posner's view, the popular self-understandings and self-descriptions we have emphasized above are in fact widespread *misunderstandings* and *flawed descriptions*. Hence his realism commits him not only to the homely view that democracy is a kind of market (2003: 166), but also to the more astonishing claim that the general populace in American society is highly deluded about the nature of its own political behavior. However, the claim that millions of people are deeply benighted with respect to their own motives surely involves the kind of theorizing that everyday pragmatists attempt to avoid. More importantly, it is the kind of claim that stands in need of exposition. This is why many expressions of democratic realism include complex and sophisticated theories of propaganda and ideological manipulation (Lippmann 1922; Chomsky and Herman 2002).

In this sense, democratic realism involves something much more robust than the simple description of democracy as market-like. It harbors an account of the citizen's political motivation and activity that seems at odds with many of our political practices. To repeat, the realist depiction renders the common democratic practice of political discussion and debate nonsensical. Posner may certainly endorse such an estimation of our practice; however, insofar as everyday pragmatism is opposed to ostentatious theorizing, academic abstraction, and detached speculation, it is an awkward companion for democratic realism. It is debatable whether democratic realism is a viable political theory, but it is in any case not a pragmatist theory in Posner's sense of the term.

EPISTEMIC DELIBERATIVISM

Democracy and Epistemology?

Thus far, we have reviewed three distinct pragmatist conceptions of democracy. The first two – Deweyan democracy and Rortyan democracy, respectively – are *aspirational* theories insofar as they hold that democracy is, at least in part, a mode of social organization in which certain moral ideals and attitudes – growth in the case of Dewey and hope in the case of Rorty – are promoted. Posner's minimalism rejects the very idea of an aspirational political theory; according to Posner, democracy is simply a kind of market arrangement in which a populace selects its rulers from among a class of elites. Cheryl Misak has developed a compelling conception deliberative democracy based in Peircean pragmatism, specifically, drawing upon features of Peirce's epistemology in devising a conception of democracy that we shall call 'epistemic deliberativism'. In this section, we will first lay out the basic features of Misak's view. Then we will draw out some implications of her view. Finally, we will raise some difficulties for epistemic deliberativism. Before embarking, however, it might be helpful to call attention to some general features of Misak's project.

Misak offers the following succinct encapsulation of her view: 'deliberative democracy in political philosophy is the right view, because deliberative democracy in epistemology is the right view' (2004b: 15).

Misak's claim should give us pause. Taken most generally, her statement alleges that political philosophy should be driven by epistemology. This is, to be sure, a deliberately dramatic reversal of Rorty's view that democratic politics should be taken to be 'prior' to philosophical theorizing. But it also marks an important departure from the most common view of the relation of political philosophy to other areas of philosophy, which holds that political theory should be driven by moral theory. That is, according to the most common conceptions, democracy is the preferred mode of political association because it alone realizes or respects some decidedly *moral* value, such as equality or liberty or autonomy. On such views, the defense of democracy follows from the defense of the moral value that democracy is said to most fully realize; we should be democrats because we are morally bound to treat each other as equals, or preserve individual liberty, or respect autonomy, and democracy alone can do this.

Misak's proposal is novel because it attempts to build a conception of democracy from certain epistemological concerns. More precisely, it says that our political philosophy should be determined by our epistemology – the right epistemology tells us what the right politics is. But notice that there's a danger lurking: the view that politics should be determined by epistemology is precisely what drives many of the standard antidemocratic views. Consider, for example, the argument commonly associated with Plato that democracy is unjust because it gives to the foolish and ignorant the same proportion of political power that it gives to the wise. The argument continues that since the wise are relatively few in number and the foolish are relatively many in number, democracy is the rule over the wise by the foolish. How could *that* be just? Famously, Plato proposed in his *Republic* that cities should be ruled by people with wisdom, who he identified as Philosopher Kings. In Plato's ideal society, the wise philosophers would rule every aspect of society; they would determine not only the laws and policies of the government, but also the intimate details of each citizen's life, what occupation he or she would take up, who he or she would marry, how many children they would have, and so on. Accordingly, many regard Plato as the archenemy of democracy.[16] We may call Plato's view *epistemarchy*, rule of those who know.[17]

But we needn't look to a radical antidemocrat like Plato to get a sense of the danger posed by the kind of thought driving Misak's position. One of Philosophy's most celebrated defenders of liberty and individuality, John Stuart Mill, comes frightfully close to endorsing epistemarchy. In his 1861 *Considerations on Representative Government*, Mill proposes that, in a democracy, those citizens who exercise their 'superior functions' or who are 'graduates of universities' should be granted 'two or more votes' at the polls (1991/1861: 336). Should this strike you as objectionable, consider that Mill goes further to say that,

> No one but a fool, and a fool of a peculiar description, feels offended by the acknowledgement that there are others whose opinion, and even whose wish, is entitled to a greater amount of consideration than his. (1991/1861: 335)

Indeed, Mill contends that this scheme of weighted voting, which is designed to 'preserve the educated from the class legislation of the uneducated', is the 'true ideal' of democracy (1991/1861: 337). Now, Mill falls short of endorsing full-blown epistemarchy, since he holds that every citizen, regardless of intellectual ability, must be given at least one vote. However, he, like Plato, denies the democratic principle of distributing political power equally. Thus we might say that Mill is a *mild* epistemarchist. And mild epistemarchy seems objectionable enough.

Mill is driven to mild epistemarchy in roughly the same way that Plato is driven to his full-blown epistemarchy: they both begin with the idea that the choice-worthiness of a form of government depends upon the *quality of its collective decisions*. For Plato, the justice of a political order depends on its ability to institute wise policies; similarly, for Mill, 'Conduciveness to Progress' is the 'whole excellence of a government' (1991/1861: 223). And here's the rub: once we identify the appropriateness of a political order with the ability of that order to produce outcomes having a certain quality, we will always be able to devise some patently nondemocratic process that more reliably produces outcomes of that sort. All we would need to do is to devise a system that gives the political power to those who know best how to secure results with the desired quality. Epistemarchy looms.

Indeed, this is precisely why most contemporary political theorists look to moral theory rather than epistemology to ground their conception of democracy. The idea is to focus on the *moral character of the democratic process* rather than the quality of its outcomes. Again, the process is justified by way of appeal to some *moral* requirement that it satisfies, such as equality. Consequently, the most common approach holds that democracy is the best or most just political order despite the fact that democracies often make bad decisions; on such views, the bestness or justice of democracy consists in the fact that its decision procedure treats individuals as they should be treated, namely, as citizens rather than as subordinates or as mere subjects.

Of course, there is much more to say about these topics. More importantly, we have not considered Misak's position in any detail yet, so we must not dismiss it on the basis of what has been said thus far. However, the summarizing sentence with which we began – 'deliberative democracy in political philosophy is the right view, because deliberative democracy in epistemology is the right view' (2004b: 15) – seems especially inviting of the kind of worry we have raised. Presumably, if 'deliberative democracy' is the right view in epistemology, it must be because deliberative democracy is the best way to achieve what we aspire to achieve as epistemic agents, namely true beliefs and the avoidance or correction of false beliefs. But, again, if acquiring truth and avoiding falsehood is our goal, then it seems easy to imagine some nondemocratic process that could more reliably produce the desired result. And so we're back to epistemarchy!

As it turns out, this kind of criticism is too hasty. Misak has a way to avoid the implication to epistemarchy. To see this, we need to look carefully at her view, beginning with her Peircean epistemology.

Fundamentals of Misak's Epistemology

Misak's politics proceeds from a particular interpretation of Peirce's epistemology. Specifically, Misak promotes a novel interpretation of Peirce's view about truth. As we saw in our chapter about pragmatist epistemology, Peirce held that 'The opinion which is fated to be ultimately agreed to be all who investigate, is what we mean by truth' (CP, 5.407). You will remember the many serious difficulties that this idea, taken as a *definition* of truth, faces. However, Misak argues that Peirce did not think that truth was to be *defined* as the belief that would be adopted by inquirers at the ideal end of inquiry. In fact, Misak claims that Peirce did not think that truth could be *defined* at all. She says that Peirce's characterization of truth is intended to help us to 'get leverage on the concept, or a fix on it, by exploring its connections with practice' (Misak 2004: viii). That is, according to Misak, Peirce aims to *clarify* or *elucidate* the concept of truth, not *define* it.

The core of Peirce's elucidation of the concept of truth is the intuitive thought that to take a proposition, p, to be true – that is, to believe that p or assert that p – is to hold that p would forever stand up to the test of experience and never be overrun or defeated. Accordingly, Misak interprets Peirce's remarks about truth as making the following recommendation:

> We should think of a true belief as a belief that would forever be assertable; a belief which would never lead to disappointment; a belief which would be 'indefeasible' or not defeated, were inquiry pursued as far as it could fruitfully go. (2004: ix)

Elsewhere, Misak expresses the thought as follows:

> The core of the pragmatist conception of truth is that a true belief would be the best belief, were we to inquire as far as we could on the matter . . . A true belief . . . is a belief that could not be improved upon, a belief that would forever meet the challenges of reasons, argument, and evidence. (2000: 49)

Thus, Misak preserves the Peircean insight that belief is intrinsically tied to inquiry. Since believing that p is taking p to be true, and taking p to be true is to take p to be able to withstand the tests and travails of ongoing scrutiny, every believer is committed to being open to *inquiry*, the enterprise of squaring one's belief with reasons, arguments, and evidence by continually subjecting one's beliefs to objections and challenges. Indeed, Misak holds that the kind of responsiveness to reasons that inquiry is meant to secure is a *constitutive norm* of belief. Misak writes,

> A belief, in order to be a belief, is such that it is responsive to reasons and evidence. That is a very part of what it is to have a belief – a *constitutive norm* of belief is that a belief is something that one holds for reasons . . . Some cognitive states – those not appropriately connected to reasons – are not deserving of the label 'belief'. (2004b: 12; italic in the original)

To be sure, Misak's claim that reason-responsiveness is a constitutive norm of belief does *not* commit her to the view that no one ever holds beliefs for defective reasons or for nothing worthy of the name 'reason' at all. The claim that reason-responsiveness is a constitutive norm of belief is consistent with the full range of irrational believing: prejudice, self-deception, fanaticism, dogmatism, stubbornness, wishful thinking, close-mindedness, and the like. To say that reason-responsiveness is a constitutive norm of belief is to say that when we believe *we take ourselves to be* reason-responsive. That is, we apply the pragmatic-functionalist requirements of belief to ourselves–when we believe, we take it that our beliefs are functionally related to evidence and the objections of those who disagree. And they are the sorts of things we will act on accordingly. Consequently, even the most closed-minded, stubborn, and fanatical believer *takes himself* to be responding to reasons. In many such cases, the believer simply has a mistaken view of what should count as a reason for his belief; nonetheless, when we believe, we take our belief to be responsive to reasons. Indeed, the constitutive norm of reason-responsiveness explains why the various forms of irrational believing often include strategies for dismissing opposition and deflating counterevidence; were reason-responsiveness not a constitutive norm, there would be no reason to evade criticism.

From these considerations, we see that Misak's Peircean epistemology is an inherently *social* epistemology. Again, to be a believer – to hold a belief – is to aim at truth. But on the Peircean view as interpreted by Misak, truth-aiming is an ineliminably *diachronic* affair: we aim at truth by always standing ready to square our beliefs with new reasons, arguments, and evidence. Indeed, to believe that *p* is to be committed to the hypothesis that *p* will stand up under scrutiny and will square with all the evidence and argument that could be brought to bear on it. Consequently, believing 'involves being prepared to try to justify one's views to others and being prepared to test one's beliefs against the experience of others' (Misak 2000: 94). For if we do not take seriously the arguments and criticisms of others, getting 'the best or the true belief is not on the cards' (Misak 2000: 94).

Accordingly, Misak holds, with Peirce, that in order to aim at truth, believers must have access to and participate in a *community* of inquirers. To explain: We have said that beliefs aim at truth and therefore believers must be responsive to reasons. But reason-responsiveness in part requires reason *exchanging*; that is, one cannot aim at truth or inquire in isolation from others. Further, since inquiry requires that what gets exchanged are *reasons* rather than slogans, insults, threats, or blows, one cannot be a proper inquirer in the absence of *other inquirers.* Hence a *community* of inquirers is necessary for there to be *individuals* who are inquirers. Consequently, the very nature of belief commits us to processes of inquiry, which in turn commits us to participation in a certain kind of community, namely one in which inquiry can commence.

From Epistemology to Democracy

We are now well positioned to see how Misak's conception of democracy emerges out of her Peircean social epistemology. According to Misak, to hold beliefs at all is to be committed to inquiry, and thus to social processes of 'debate and deliberation' (2000: 106) with others. These commitments entail a range of interpersonal norms that Misak sees as characteristically democratic. Specifically, Misak contends that the commitment to the enterprise of justification entails that one must subject one's beliefs to objections and challenges *from all quarters*, since 'anyone might be an expert' (2000: 96) and anyone might have a relevant countervailing consideration or counterargument. Consequently, we must stand ready to 'listen to others' (2000: 96) and take their arguments and experiences seriously. Perhaps more importantly, inquiry commits us to engaging with those whose experiences differ from our own; for if we are aiming at truth, we must seek out new and unfamiliar challenges. In this way, the norms of belief entail interpersonal norms of equality, participation, recognition, and inclusion.

From these interpersonal norms, a range of social norms emerges. In order for individuals to exchange reasons and collectively inquire, there must be norms of free speech, freedom of information, open debate, protected dissent, accountability, and so on. Additionally, if inquiry is to commence, the formal infrastructure of democracy must be in place, including a constitution, courts, accountable bodies of representation, regular elections, and a free press. Also, there must be a system of public schooling designed to equip students in the epistemic habits necessary for inquiry, and institutions of distributive justice to eliminate as far as justice allows the material obstructions to democratic citizenship. Further, democracy *might* also require more extensive provisions, such as special measures to preserve public spaces and to create forums for citizens to encounter new perspectives.

The important point is that Misak holds that the full range of democratic norms, from the interpersonal to the social and institutional, can be derived from her pragmatist epistemology. Hence Misak argues that *opponents* of democracy – tyrants, authoritarians, and the like – are committing a kind of error. Misak argues that the tyrant, insofar as she holds beliefs at all, 'is committed to having her beliefs governed by reasons' (2000: 160), and so 'is committed, whether [she] acknowledges it or not' to the norms of inquiry, which, as we have seen entail democratic norms (2000: 106). That is, Misak contends that opponents of democracy are caught in a kind of *epistemic bad faith*: They uphold a political order which is inconsistent with *their own* epistemic commitments.

Avoiding Epistemarchy

Here is where we find resources in Misak's view for blocking the implication to epistemarchy. Recall the problem: Once we adopt the idea that the justification of democracy lies in its ability to produce wise, rational, or truth-tracking outcomes, we are confronted with the likelihood that some nondemocratic process is *better* at producing outcomes of that sort than democracy is. Misak avoids epistemarchy by appealing to the epistemic properties of democracy *not* at the level of the quality of democratic outcomes, but at the level of the epistemic norms that are internal to belief and inquiry. That is, unlike Plato and Mill, Misak does not assert that the value of a political order is to be determined by the epistemic value of its policies and decisions; rather, she contends that democracy is the social and political manifestation of the epistemic norms which govern our cognitive lives. In this way, on Misak's view, democracy is not proposed as an *instrument* to wise policy, but as the social and political *counterpart* to our epistemic commitments. According to Misak, we must endorse democratic norms because only in a democracy can we live up to our epistemic commitments; that is, only in a democracy can we be inquirers.

Given this, a stronger conclusion follows. From Misak's perspective, epistemarchy is incoherent. This is most obvious in the case of full-blown epistemarchy advocated by Plato. Recall that the Platonic epistemarchist holds that the best political order is one in which total political power resides in the hands of Philosopher Kings, those who have total knowledge. According to Misak, there are no knowers of the sort envisioned by the Platonic epistemarchist. Since, on Misak's Peircean view, truth itself is not a static property of a proposition, but rather a matter of a proposition's ability to withstand the ongoing tests of inquiry, knowledge is not a fixed state of a mind which with justification believes a true proposition; rather, on Misak's view, knowledge must be something more like the *skill* of inquiring, the skill of meeting objections and overcoming potential defeaters to one's belief. If knowledge is something like the ability to skillfully inquire, then all knowers are implicitly committed to the democratic norms we discussed above; consequently, no knower could endorse epistemarchy, for epistemarchy is inconsistent with knowing.

From Epistemology to Democracy?

Our discussion of how Misak avoids the implication to epistemarchy provides a good occasion for raising difficulties with her epistemic deliberativism. Perhaps the main worry is that Misak attempts to derive too much substance from the very meager insights from which she begins. Recall that Misak's claim is that an entire conception of democratic politics can be derived from a few truisms of epistemology. Is this plausible? Here's one objection: Let us grant Misak's claim that the norms that govern belief commit us to inquiry, which in turn commits us to taking each other's reasons seriously. We may even grant further that taking each other's reasons seriously commits us to norms of inclusiveness, participation, and equality. But these are not sufficient for a democratic society, for seeing others as equal partners in inquiry is consistent with seeing those same others as *political* subordinates. That is, it seems fully consistent with Misak's epistemology for one to regard his fellow believers as *consultants*, whose arguments and objections have merely *recommendatory* force, rather than as *political equals* who are entitled to *equal* political power and *equal* influence over political decision. Another way of putting the concern is this: Misak may be able to avoid full-blown epistemarchy endorsed by Plato, but can she avoid the *mild* epistemarchy of Mill? What in her epistemology blocks Millian weighted voting? What on her view is objectionable about arrangements that give all people access to social processes of reason exchange, but restrict the power of collective decision to only a few? Is something crucial to the idea of a democratic society lost if Misak cannot give an *in principle* defense of the equal distribution of political power?

Perhaps Misak would respond that in order for inquiry to truly commence, the upshot of inquiry must have political force. The way to ensure that inquiry has such force, Misak may argue, is to give to all believers an equal vote. Yet this kind of reply gives rise to another worry. If democracy is the political upshot of our epistemic commitment to aim at truth, and if we want our politics to reflect the outcomes of our inquiries, then what justification could there be for the *democratic nation-state*? Why shouldn't persons who live in, say, Italy be consulted on questions concerning political policy in, say, Canada? Surely people in Italy are inquirers and will have a distinctive view of Canadian politics. If the point of democracy is to have policy reflect our best reasons, then why should political power within a given state be restricted to those who happen to live within its borders? Does Misak's view entail a *global* democracy, a democracy without sovereign nations?

These institutional concerns may be met with considerations of a purely practical nature. Misak may say that a global democracy is impractical, and that, for better or worse, we are stuck with the nation-state. Perhaps she would be correct to say this. But the thought of a world governed by global inquiry raises a different kind of worry, one addressed to Misak's social epistemology rather than its institutional upshots. Recall that Misak thinks that believing commits us to norms of reason exchanging such that to believe that *p* is to stand ready to offer reasons why *p* is true and respond to arguments against *p*. The worry is that Misak has glossed over crucial issues: What is to count as a reason for *p*? What is to count as an argument against *p*? Very frequently disagreements over moral and political matters seem to be, at last in part, disagreements about the precise meaning of our epistemic commitments. In particular, many moral and political controversies involve disagreements about what should count as *evidence* for a given proposition. To take an easy example, some democratic citizens hold that the fact that the Bible condemns homosexuality constitutes *evidence*, and perhaps *conclusive evidence*, that homosexuality is immoral; some further hold that the fact that homosexuality is immoral constitutes evidence – again, perhaps *conclusive* evidence – that homosexuality should be criminalized, or, at the very least, *discouraged* by the state. Of course, there are lots of citizens who hold that the Bible is irrelevant. To use a different kind of case, some take statistics concerning gun-related crime to constitute evidence for stricter gun-control policies, whereas others think that even a very high incidence of gun-related crime is beside the point.

It would be easy to multiply examples of this sort. The point is that, even if we grant Misak's core epistemic claims – namely, that beliefs aim at truth, and aiming at truth involves being responsive to reasons, evidence, and argument – we still may disagree in specific cases about whether some statement, *s*, counts as *evidence* for, or is a reason in favor of, *p*. So, although we may all agree with Misak's *description* of the norms governing belief, we may yet be in conflict regarding the *content* of these norms. And how are such conflicts to be resolved? To say that we should exchange our reasons is to make no progress, since we are divided over what should count as a reason. Some would say that we should look to the empirical sciences for guidance; others would say that we should follow our commonsense intuitions; some would recommend that we *pray* for the right answer or *consult a sacred book*; still others would say that we should give up on the very idea of epistemic criteria. What could count as a reason to adopt one of these answers rather than another?

If the commitment to inquiry is going to form the core of our conception of democracy, we had better get specific about what we mean by *inquiry* and the related notions, *evidence*, *argument*, and *reason*. The trouble, however, is this: Once Misak provides the requisite details – once she says what she means by *evidence* and the rest – her description of the norms of belief will likely lose their intuitive resonance. But it is the intuitive character of her views about the tight connections between belief, argument, reason, and evidence that accounts for much of the appeal of her epistemic deliberativism.

CHAPTER 7

PRAGMATISM AND ENVIRONMENTAL ETHICS

ENVIRONMENTAL ETHICS AND ITS DISCONTENTS

Moral Ontology

In this concluding chapter, we take up one of the many overtly 'applied' issues in philosophy. Pragmatism clearly has application to many issues in contemporary environmental philosophy, since the tradition's methods are designed to address many of the concerns of public policy, value, and the consequences of human actions.

An organizing issue in environmental philosophy is that of *moral ontology*: What beings count morally? What are the things we should treat as objects of moral concern? Answers to the question come in different varieties, but they may be divided into two broad camps: the *anthropocentric* and the *nonanthropocentric*. Anthropocentrists hold that humans are the only morally valuable things, and nonanthropocentrists hold that there are other beings beyond humans that deserve moral concern. Animals, for example, can be of moral concern because of their capacity to feel pain and pleasure. Or they may lay a claim on us by the fact that their lives should be allowed to continue and flourish undisturbed. But if life's flourishing is valuable, perhaps plants and trees, too, deserve a measure of moral consideration. Call this broad subgroup of nonanthropocentrists the *biocentrists*. Further, consider the health and functioning of a whole ecosystem or planet, including its dirt, rocks, water, and gasses. Could these things be of moral concern? Call answers in the affirmative *ecocentrist*. The question, then, is how wide should the boundaries of moral concern be drawn? Should it have a small group inside (humans, or maybe a small subgroup of them) or should it encompass everything? How does one draw such a line?

How and where the line is drawn does not necessarily preclude attitudes of environmental conservation and concern. Immanuel Kant held that rational beings were the proper objects of moral concern, but it did not follow that one may treat animals in any way one likes. Instead, he reasoned, one has an *indirect duty* to animals because mistreating animals is conducive of mistreating people (1963: 239–40). The same reasoning may be applied to wider environmental concerns – for example, littering does not respect the integrity of a piece of land, and as a consequence, it is productive of or a manifestation of a broader tendency not to respect dignity in humans. Additionally, anthropocentrists may find positive reasons to treat the environment as though it were intrinsically valuable, perhaps for their own good because environments demand such respect in order for us to get what we want from them. Think, for example, of national parks. It is better to treat them as though they are intrinsically valuable. That way, they will be just right for the times we go to enjoy them or when wildlife photographers go there. The same, as we are finding, goes for rainforests, lakes, oceans, and so on. In order to get what we want and need from them (clean water, places for our waste to be absorbed efficiently, good harvests), we must treat them more and more carefully. For societies to be viable, they must be cognizant of their environs. For the anthropocentrist, nature is of an instrumental value, but a value nonetheless.

To the nonanthropocentrist, this sounds very much like selfishness, if not tempered greed. Especially when seen from the perspective of an environment, nature as a whole, or from the view of other animals trying to live, anthropocentric valuing and policy making is a form of *speciesism* – taking one species' values to be more important than those of the others for no other reason than that one can. Saying that one should clean up a lake so that one can drink its water and harvest its fish is akin to treating other humans nicely and ensuring they are taken care of so that they will make good slaves. That is, the slave owner who treats his slaves decently and ensures their health is surely preferable to one who does not, but he nevertheless is a slave owner. If nature, environments, forests, or populations of nonhuman animals are objects of moral concern in their own right, then anthropocentric conservationism is better than many alternatives, but it is nevertheless morally corrupt.

Pragmatist have sought to help with two main issues within the area of moral ontology. The first is with the *metaphysics*: pragmatist methods are uniquely designed to address and reconstruct metaphysical disputes. The second is with the *politics*: given the depth of disagreement and contestability of the conceptions of good environmental policy, pragmatism's meliorism and democratic commitments (surveyed in the previous chapters) may alleviate the tensions. We will address these two issues separately.

RECONSTRUCTED ENVIRONMENTAL METAPHYSICS

The Reconstructive Pragmatist Program

Pragmatist naturalism is posited on the thought that humans are animals responding to and coping with their environments. As a consequence, much of human life is a product of this interaction. Human goals, values, and experiences are results of such ongoing exchange. Applying Dewey's conception of naturalism, Larry Hickman notes that nature provides:

> Experiences and experiments, unanticipated events, chance insights, moments of aesthetic ecstasy, habits, traditions, and institutions. (1996: 53)

In turn, humans reformulate and anticipate these natural outgrowths of embodied life with religion, commentary, poetry, art, and philosophy. Humans are designed to be attuned to the environment. We not only grasp certain facts about the world around us, but we also live immersed within it. As a consequence, we are engaged with it (Rosenthal and Buchholz 1996: 43). As Kelly Parker notes, 'the human sphere is embedded at every point in the natural sphere' (1996: 21).

The promise of pragmatism in metaphysics is the naturalistic reconstruction of the old theoretical divides so that one may resolve the disputes empirically and continue with things that matter. In the case of environmental philosophy, what matters is protection of ecosystems. It is not unusual for articles written on any side of the moral ontology debate to end with a pragmatic flourish, one that reminds us that there is *work* to be done, not more *philosophy* to be written. The forests are burning while we debate some finer point of metaphysics.

Pragmatic reconstruction, then, should serve dual purposes. On the one hand, it should resolve or dissolve the theoretical problems dividing otherwise like-minded people. And so, the engaged-in-the-environment model is proposed as a solution. It is a kind of synthesis of anthropocentric and nonanthropocentric views, one that accommodates the human perspective, but also puts it in a broader view of things. On the other hand, pragmatist reconstruction is a practical move wherein we not only bridge the theoretical gaps dividing theorists and activists alike, but in so bridging the gap, we refocus people on solving real problems. Pragmatism entails a clear view of what is needed for environmental responsibility (Holden 2001: 54).

The central notion of pragmatic reconstruction of environmental philosophy and ethics generally is that of *growth*. As we noted earlier in the chapters on ethics and politics, growth is a central value for Deweyan pragmatism. Dewey regards growth as a biological phenomenon, one that is posited on the flourishing of an organism. Dewey takes it that growth is a goal of constant reconstruction:

> The reality *is* the growth process itself; childhood and adulthood are phases of a continuity, in which just because it is a history, the latter cannot exist until the former exists . . .; and in which the latter makes use of the registered and cumulative outcome of the earlier–or, more strictly, *is* its utilization. (LW1: 210)

For the reconstructionist program, growth is a moral imperative, one that requires that we expand our cultural horizons, broaden the variety and richness of our practices, and make the world a place where others may pursue those goals, too (Rosenthal and Buchholz 1996: 42; Holden 2001: 51).

Critics of Pragmatist Environmental Philosophy

The goal of growth, on its face, seems to be diametrically opposed to conservation and preservation. If growth is the central goal, then one should con- or pre-serve only as much as is required for later growth. C. A. Bowers, in criticizing the pragmatist reconstructive program, notes:

> [Pragmatist] epistemology, with its emphasis on growth in the capacity to reconstruct experience . . . would represent yet another expression of Western colonialism . . . [that] would further undermine the ability of many cultures to avoid the consumer/technology

dependent lifestyle that is one of the major contributors to the ecological crisis. (2003: 26)

Cultural, political, and technological growth, Bowers reasons, places Deweyan-pragmatist thought squarely on the side not only of anthropocentrist views (and hence, as failed attempts to bridge the gap with nonanthropocentrism), but also on the side of the interests of first-world capitalists. The focus on growth, reconstruction, and their changes promotes a scaled view of culture, and so, Bowers takes it, the program 'marginalizes the various forms of knowledge that characterize many indigenous cultures that have learned to live with the sustainable limits of their bioregions' (2003: 33). That is, pragmatist reconstruction is imperialist not only in terms of looking at the land as a resource for further growth, but it is imperialist in reconstructing cultures. Pragmatism, with its emphasis on growth and its use of reconstructive means pursuant of growth, is less the answer to the problems facing environmental philosophy, but rather is the embodiment of the problems.

The pragmatist response is that growth may require, in these contexts, scaling back or even sacrifice. Defending the pragmatist account, Kelly Parker notes that growth is not so gross:

'Growth' here is not reducible to 'material growth' . . . Growth might better be understood in terms of increasing the aesthetic richness of experience, of expanding the available means of finding satisfaction in life. (1996: 27)

Parker insists that these new appropriations of Deweyan metaphors need not be constrained by the industrial-capitalist histories of its use (2004: 333). As such, instead of supporting a development of material culture, expansion of markets, and growth of the gross national product, growth might require that one, as Parker put it, 'recycling one's television rather than upgrading the cable service' (1996: 27).

But now two questions hang. The first is whether the conceptions of growth Parker surveys are the only options. Is it only a choice between material and economic growth on one side and aesthetic growth on the other? Furthermore, the sacrifices Parker poses when taking the path of aesthetic growth are underplayed – it is not just a matter of [recycle] one's television or opting out of consumerist culture. For many, the choice between that of affordable goods and energy and that of opting out of such an economy is not one of growth in an aesthetic sense, but a matter of life or death for a business or family. To frame the issue as between consumerism and recycling one's television utterly misrepresents and trivializes the sacrifices necessary here. Parker does later argue that growth requires social reform in participatory democracies that respect the needs of its citizens, but on the categories for this reform, Parker is silent. The second question is whether growth in this new employment means anything at all. Parker holds that the terms themselves may be constantly reconstructed (2004: 333). If growth now means that economies must be scaled back, production must be restricted, and people must do without some goods, then so be it. The term also means expanded horizons, openness, plenitude, cosmopolitanism, complexity, and even democracy in most pragmatist deployments. The problem is that this defense against the objection that growth is inconsistent with conservation makes the term *growth* mean nothing at all. *Growth*, if it can be reconstructed to fit whatever goals need to be pursued, is inconsistent with nothing. This defense of the view evacuates it of content.

PRAGMATISM AND ENVIRONMENTAL POLITICS

The Political Divide

The second point of friction between anthropocentrists and nonanthropocentrists is how environmental policy should be developed, agreed upon, and implemented. Pragmatists hold themselves to be uniquely well positioned to mediate these disputes.

The political difficulty can be captured by the thought that if nonanthropocentric value commitments demand that many human agents ignore if not hold in positive contempt the objections of their fellow humans, there will most certainly be political strife. In fact, it seems that the conditions for democracy (any other stable political order) are threatened. Take, for example, Arne Naess claiming that the deep ecology movement is posited on a 'rejection of the man-in-environment image in favor of a relational field-image' (1973). What this field image requires of us politically is to pursue the preservation of wildernesses and other ecosystems. To pursue these policy ends, Naess insists that deep ecologists must 'reject the monopoly of narrowly human and short-term argument patterns in favor of long-term arguments' (1995: 452). One must adopt a quasireligious view of the world and its ecosystems and pursue policies in light of these commitments. As deep ecologists see it, the process of framing the policies in ways other people who do not share this religious vision can understand is an unacceptable restriction on the requirements of deep ecology. Similarly, Aldo Leopold proposes a vision of how environments hang together and are valuable as complete wholes with his Land Ethic. On Leopold's analysis, economic and other anthropocentric forms of land conservation are short-sighted and all too weakly motivating to be effective (1977/1949: 108). What is necessary, Leopold holds, is that education (especially with farmers) be reformed so that 'one enlarges the boundaries of the community to include soils, waters, plants, animals, or collectively: the land' (1977/1949: 103). The land ethic has it that all obligations derive directly from an individual's place in the community of the earth as a whole. People need to be reeducated, Leopold contends, so they understand this. Motivating them or arguing with them on any other basis is not worthwhile.

Of course, with both of these programs, those in the opposition, the anthropocentrists, are treated with a form of intellectual contempt – one need not *argue with them* politically, but rather, one argues over them or educates them. Those who oppose deep ecology or the land ethic are conceived of as people who live under a kind of cognitive haze that must be dispelled with consciousness raising or browbeating.

From a pragmatist perspective, these programs are objectionable for two reasons. The first is their intellectual arrogance, as the default is to take it that those who disagree are not reasonable. Instead, intellectual resistance is a consequence of some defect, vice, or ignorance that must be corrected. These views run afoul of fallibilism. The second problem is that if one subscribes to these accounts, one does not have critical discussions with those with whom one does not agree, but rather one converts, educates, or berates them. This not only makes for positively toxic rhetoric, but also risks antidemocratic politics.

Pragmatist Reconstructed Politics

A pragmatist strategy has been proposed here by Andrew Light as 'compatibilism in political ecology'. Light argues that if liberal democracies are to pass legislation and fix policies that address environmental concerns, the arguments given for any of the laws must meet the demands of *the principle of tolerance.* The demands of tolerance are that those holding a policy as right must communicate a 'straightforward public position', one that reflects the considerations of all involved and thereby is best suited to meeting their 'mutually desired goods' (1996: 170–1). Values and goals that do not live up to this are *private,* and they are goals one may pursue on one's own. Given the familiar liberal public–private distinction, Light argues that pragmatists are not 'wedded to any particular theoretical framework . . . they can choose the avenue which best protects the long-term health and stability of the environment, regardless of its theoretical origin' (1996: 172).

Bryan Norton poses a similar pragmatic strategy of bridging the political chasms of theoretical disagreement. The problem is that both anthropocentrism and nonanthropocentrism are posited on monistic theories of value – they take only one source of value to be legitimate (1996: 106). He proposes that public discussion of environmental policy integrates three perspectives of concern and value: (a) those of individual humans, (b) those of human and ecological communities, and (c) global values that reflect the long-term prospects for the survival of the human species and the broader environment (1996: 127–8). Norton holds that this requirement of integrated viewpoints is both more likely to be successful in being agreed upon by a valuationally pluralistic populace and more likely to avoid having to exclude anyone's views from consideration (1996: 132; cf. Mintz 2004). The point, as Norton reasons, is that 'theoretical disagreements often need not impede developing current policy; if all disputants agree on central management principles' (1996: 108).

The difficulties faced for these pragmatist strategies of compatibilism and integration is that for many people involved in the debates, the values they care about in the dispute are the only or the singularly most important values on the table. To square them against values they not only may not care about but may also hold in full contempt is perhaps too much to ask. Moreover, to keep their own most deeply held views private or measured on another scale *perverts* those values. Holding arguers to the requirement of tolerance or integration certainly puts people who disagree into a more respectful and civil relation, and the prospects of resolution are good. *But getting people there* requires that they think that pragmatist reconstructions of not only the public sphere are right, but also pragmatic reconstructions of the goods they are committed to are right. For example, on Light's view, for the deep ecologist to live up to the requirements of tolerance, she must hold that her views on the value of the whole of the environment and what must be done in the name of it are really *private values*, as opposed to *public issues*. The problem is that of the eight principles of deep ecology, many are about the public sphere and how human civilization needs change:

4. The flourishing of human life is compatible with a substantial decrease of the human population. The flourishing of non-human life requires such a decrease.
6. The dominant socio-political living situation must therefore end. This will affect basic economic, technological, and ideological structures. The resulting state of affairs will be deeply different from the present. (Devall and Sessions 1985: 70)

Finally, note that the last principle of deep ecology is that deep ecologists are duty-bound to pursue these goals:

8. Those who subscribe to the foregoing points have an obligation to directly or indirectly implement the necessary changes. (Devall and Sessions 1985: 70)

Light's requirement of tolerance, then, is equivalent to the prohibition of any contentious political or ethical views being brought out for public discussion. This, surely, will bring consensus, but it will be a false one, since the views that generate the disagreements to begin with are the contentious ones. The only way a deep ecologist would accept such a requirement for her participation in public debate would be if she were a liberal pragmatist first. In this respect, pragmatist compatibilism is achieved by holding that all the differences the people have don't really matter, and requiring that *they* think that the differences don't matter, too.

In similar fashion, Norton's strategy of integrating the various conflicting views on a scalar model reflecting the pluralism of the values to be maximized suffers from the fact that not all the people the model applies to will be pluralists. Surely it is better to use the model if one is a pluralist, but the model of integration is no solution for those who are nevertheless what Norton terms 'monists' regarding environmental value (1996: 132). What is required is that those in the debates adopt a pragmatic-pluralist attitude toward their values before they step in the door. But the people in these disagreements aren't pragmatists. They are deep ecologists, land ethicists, animal liberationists, and conservationists. The fact that they disagree heatedly shows that they aren't liberal pragmatists first. In fact, many involved in these debates hold that the liberal pragmatist categories of public, private, and plural are not a solution to the problem but a positive hindrance to any solution. Resisting similar constraints, Adam Briggle and Robert Frodeman argue that 'to promote a strict dividing line [between public and private] at some point becomes less a defense of reason than an irrational exclusion of many of the ethical and philosophical commitments that motivate us' (2006: 60). Robert Goodin goes further and holds that the pluralist liberal democratic norms should be secondary to core environmental commitments – if liberal democracy cannot efficiently achieve the ends that must be achieved, so much the worse for it (1992: 100). Unless the categories driving Light's compatibilism and Norton's integration can be reconstructed in lights nonpragmatists can agree to, the solutions are likely as contentious as the disagreements they are supposed to solve.

NOTES

CHAPTER 1: THE ORIGINS OF PRAGMATISM

1. Citations to Peirce's writing will be keyed to *The Collected Papers of Charles Sanders Peirce* (Hartshorne, Weiss, and Burks, eds) and will employ the standard formula: (CP, volume number.paragraph number).
2. Citations to James's writing will be keyed to *The Writings of William James* (James 1977) and will employ the abbreviation 'WWJ'.
3. 'Proposition' is intended at present to denote that which bears a truth value, whatever that might be. Hence we do not mean to imply a distinction between propositions, and, say, sentences or utterances or statements or expressions; nor do we mean to commit to any particular view of the relations between propositions and these other linguistic items. We shall introduce the usual distinctions later in this book. For now, 'proposition' strikes us as a more appropriate term than Peirce's own 'idea', 'thought', or 'concept', all of which tend to carry unwanted mentalistic connotations.
4. Peirce initially expressed these points in the form of indicative conditionals, which led him to adopt the overly nominalistic view that no diamond is hard until it is actually rubbed against another object (CP, 5.403). He later revised this view and accepted the subjunctive formulation employed above (see CP, 8.208).
5. Peirce claims that there is a rule that 'deserves to be inscribed upon every wall of the city of philosophy: Do not block the way of inquiry' (CP, 1.135).
6. References to Dewey's work will be keyed to the 37-volume *Collected Works* and will employ the standard formula: (volume number: page number).
7. In 'How to Make Our Ideas Clear', Peirce refers to 'The Fixation of Belief' as 'the first part of this essay' (CP, 5.394).
8. See especially Dewey's 1938 *Logic: The Theory of Inquiry* (LW12), and also his 1910 *How We Think* (MW6); in addition, see the pivotal early essays 'The Reflex Arc Concept in Psychology' of 1896 (EW5: 96–109) and 'Some Stages of Logical Thought' of 1900 (EW1: 151–74).
9. Here, Peirce means 'science' in the broadest possible sense; it is the method which 'goes out of its way to test hypotheses by experiment' (Misak 2004a: 80).

¹⁰ Cf. Hookway, 'Reflection on four competing methods of inquiry shows that only one of them is capable of being sustained' (2002: 34).
¹¹ See Dicker (1976: ch. 4) for a sympathetic review of the controversy and an attempt to render Dewey's view plausible. See also Thayer (1952: 161ff.; 1993), Tiles (1988: ch. 5), and Burke (1994).

CHAPTER 2: PRAGMATISM AND EPISTEMOLOGY

¹ Thomas McCarthy makes a version of this argument against cognitive relativism in 'Contra Relativism: A Thought Experiment': 'Some differences [between languages, cultures, epistemic systems] are more than differences, because they can be best understood as the result of learning' (1989: 265).
² For a similar list of desiderata for epistemological theories, see Paul Boghossian (2006: 39–41).
³ Susan Haack calls this the 'passes for' fallacy (1998: 117–18).
⁴ We will discuss reflective equilibrium in slightly more depth in Chapter 5.
⁵ For further reading on Howell's puzzle for epistemic pragmatism, see Phillips (2007) and Aikin (2007).

CHAPTER 3: PRAGMATISM AND TRUTH

¹ This thought has been echoed by Mark Johnston (1993) and Jeffrey Stout (2007).
² This argument has been made by William Alston (1996: 258), Alvin Goldman (1999: 72–3), and Michael Lynch (2005: 92).
³ Michael Lynch makes a similar argument (2005: 93).

CHAPTER 4: PRAGMATISM AND METAPHYSICS

¹ For accounts of pragmatist versions of naturalist methodology, see Quine (1969), Capps (1996), Rosenthal (1996), Godfrey-Smith (2002), and Aikin (2005).
² A formal version of this problem for confirmation or disconfirmation of theories is called the Quine–Duhem thesis. This thesis holds that empirical evidence is not always so simple because one's experience is the arbiter for one's theories only because one adopts certain theories to assess what evidence one's experience provides. See Quine (1951/1961) and Duhem (1954).
³ See Aikin and Hodges (2006: 12–13).
⁴ This argument goes back to Descartes's *Meditations on First Philosophy* (1996/1641), but can be found in Nagel (1980) and Chalmers (1996).
⁵ See Jerry Fodor (2003: 34) and John Searle (2004: 65–6) for versions of this argument applying to pragmatism specifically (Fodor) and functionalism generally (Searle).
⁶ Or, perhaps, the sun sitting still and the earth rotating such that the viewer on earth is brought around to see the sun.

CHAPTER 5: PRAGMATISM AND ETHICS

[1] The term 'considered moral judgment' derives from John Rawls, who popularized reflective equilibrium in moral theory. See especially Rawls (1999a: 42; 1996: 8).

CHAPTER 6: PRAGMATISM AND POLITICS

[1] A fuller version of the argument of this section can be found in Talisse (2007: ch. 2). See also Talisse (2003).

[2] According to Dewey, the 'heart and guarantee of democracy is in free gatherings of neighbors on the street corner to discuss back and forth what is read in uncensored news of the day' (LW14: 227).

[3] On the social self, Dewey holds that 'The idea that individuals are born separate and isolated and are brought into society only through some artificial device is a pure myth'; he continues, 'No one is born except in dependence on others . . . The human being is an individual because of and in relation to others' (LW7: 227). Dewey also holds that 'society and individuals are correlative, organic, to one another' (MW12: 187). Contemporary Deweyan democrats maintain this commitment; see Boisvert (1998: 54f.), Green (1999: 6), Stuhr (1998: 85), Fesmire (2003: 11), and Colapietro (2006: 25).

[4] See Talisse and Aikin (2005a, 2005b) for further discussion.

[5] A more detailed version of the argument that follows can be found in Talisse (2001).

[6] Rorty identifies several such enemies; for example, Nietzsche, Loyola (Rorty 1988: 187), racists (Rorty 1996: 335), Nazis, and totalitarians (Rorty 1987: 42).

[7] For Rorty, it is enough to say of critics of democracy such as Nietzsche and Loyola that they are 'mad', 'crazy' (Rorty 1988: 187); later he advises that democrats simply 'refuse to argue' with them (Rorty 1988: 190).

[8] See also Talisse (2005, 2007: ch. 5).

[9] It is worth noting that Posner is a judge on the U.S. Court of Appeals.

[10] This description is greatly simplified – there are many distinct versions of deliberative democracy in the literature, and not all of them fix on reciprocity specifically. See Bohman (1998) and Freeman (2000) for helpful reviews of the literature. For more recent articulations, see Gutmann and Thompson (2004), Dryzek (2006), Bohman (2007), and Estlund (2008).

[11] For a comprehensive critical treatment, see Mackie (2003).

[12] Although we are speaking here particularly from within the context of the Unites States, the point is not restricted to that context.

[13] This is to say nothing about the sophistication of the deliberations that one can find on sports radio programming, where call-ins regularly have an impressive command of statistics, facts, and other data.

[14] Consider the technicality of Russell Hardin's work, much of which is squarely within the realist tradition (e.g., Hardin 2003).

[15] For expressions of such criticisms, see Macpherson (1973), Mansbridge (1983: ch. 2), Nino (1996: 79–82), Christiano (1996: 133–40), Shapiro (2003: ch. 3), Munnichis (2002).

[16] On this, see Karl Popper's classic indictment of Plato, *The Open Society and Its Enemies* (1971).

[17] Cf. Estlund (1993, 1997, 2008) who uses the term 'epistocracy' to refer to this kind of position.

REFERENCES

Aikin, Scott. 2005. 'Who's Afraid of Epistemology's Regress Problem?' *Philosophical Studies,* 126(2), 191–217.

—2006. 'Pragmatism, Naturalism, and Phenomenology'. *Human Studies,* 29, 317–40.

—2007. 'Bar Room Knowledge and Epistemic Pragmatism: A Response to Phillips'. *Southwest Philosophy Review,* 23(2).

Aikin, Scott and Hodges, Michael. 2006. 'Wittgenstein, Dewey, and the Possibility of the Religious'. *The Journal of Speculative Philosophy,* 20(1), 1–19.

Alston, William. 1996. *A Realist Conception of Truth.* Ithaca, NY: Cornell University Press.

Bernstein, Richard. 1995. 'American Philosophy: The Conflict of Narratives'. In *Rorty and Pragmatism.* Herman Saatkamp, ed. Nashville, TN: Vanderbilt University Press.

Boghossian, Paul. 2006. *Fear of Knowledge.* Oxford: Oxford University Press.

Bohman, James. 1998. 'The Coming of Age of Deliberative Democracy'. *The Journal of Political Philosophy,* 6.4, 400–25.

—2007. *Democracy across Borders.* Cambridge, MA: MIT Press.

Boisvert, Raymond. 1998. *John Dewey: Rethinking Our Time.* Albany, NY: SUNY Press.

Bowers, C. A. 2003. 'The Case against John Dewey as an Environmental and Eco-Justice Philosopher'. *Environmental Ethics,* 25(1), 25–42.

Bradley, F. H. 1963/1922. *The Principles of Logic and Terminal Essays.* Oxford: Oxford University Press.

Brandom, Robert. 1994. *Making it Explicit.* Cambridge, MA: Harvard University Press.

—2001. *Articulating Reasons.* Cambridge, MA: Harvard University Press.

Briggle, Adam and Frodeman, Robert. 2006. 'Commentary on "Democratic Deliberation, Public Reason, and Environmental Politics"'. *Environmental Philosophy,* 3(2), 59–63.

Burke, Thomas. 1994. *Dewey's New Logic.* Chicago: University of Chicago Press.

Capps, John. 1996. 'Dewey, Quine, and Pragmatic Naturalized Epistemology'. *Transactions of the Charles S. Peirce Society,* 32, 634–67.

Carnap, Rudolph. 1967/1950. 'Empiricism, Semantics, and Ontology'. In *The Linguistic Turn.* Richard Rorty, ed. Chicago: Chicago University Press. 72–84.

REFERENCES

Chalmers, David. 1996. *The Conscious Mind*. Oxford: Oxford University Press.

Chomsky, Noam and Herman, Edward. 2002. *Manufacturing Consent*. Revised edition. New York: Pantheon Books.

Christiano, Thomas. 1996. *The Rule of the Many*. Boulder, CO: Westview.

Clanton, Caleb J. 2008. *Religion and Democratic Citizenship: Inquiry and Conviction in the American Public Square*. Lanham, MD: Lexington Books.

Colapietro, Vincent. 2006. 'Democracy as a Moral Ideal'. *Kettering Review*, 24(3), 21–31.

Davidson, Donald. 1984. 'On the Very Idea of a Conceptual Scheme'. *Inquiries into Truth and Interpretation*. Oxford: Oxford University Press.

—1986. 'A Coherence Theory of Truth and Knowledge'. In *Truth and Interpretation*. Ernest Leplore, ed. New York: Blackwell. 307–19.

Descartes, Rene. 1996/1641. *Meditations on First Philosophy*. John Cottingham, ed. Cambridge: Cambridge University Press.

Devall, Bill and Sessions, George. 1985. *Deep Ecology: Living as if Nature Mattered*. Salt Lake City: Peregrine Smith.

De Waal, Cornelis. 1999. 'Eleven Challenges to the Pragmatic Theory of Truth'. *Transactions of the Charles S. Peirce Society*, 35(4), 748–66.

Dewey, John. 1969–1991. *The Collected Works of John Dewey: The Early Works, The Middle Works, The Later Works* (37 vols). Jo Ann Boydston, ed. Illinois: Southern Illinois University Press.

Dicker, Georges. 1976. *John Dewey's Theory of Knowing*. Philadelphia: Philosophical Monographs.

Dryzek, John. 2006. *Deliberative Democracy and Beyond*. New York: Oxford University Press.

Duhem, Pierre. 1954. *The Aim and Structure of Physical Theory*. Princeton, NJ: Princeton University Press.

Estlund, David. 1993. 'Making Truth Safe for Democracy'. In *The Idea of Democracy*. David Copp, Jean Hampton, and John Roemer, eds. Cambridge: Cambridge University Press. 71–100.

—1997. 'Beyond Fairness and Deliberation'. In *Deliberative Democracy*. James Bohman and William Rehg, eds. Cambridge, MA: MIT Press.

—2008. *Democratic Authority*. Princeton, NJ: Princeton University Press.

Fantl, Jeremy. 2003. 'Modest Infinitism'. *Canadian Journal of Philosophy*, 33(4), 537–62.

Fesmire, Steven. 2003. *John Dewey and Moral Imagination*. Indianapolis: Indiana University Press.

Fine, Arthur. 2007. 'Relativism, Pragmatism, and the Practice of Science'. In *The New Pragmatists*. Cheryl Misak, ed. Oxford: Oxford University Press.

Fodor, Jerry. 2003. *Hume Variations*. Oxford: Oxford University Press.

Freeman, Samuel. 2000. 'Deliberative Democracy: A Sympathetic Comment'. *Philosophy and Public Affairs*, 29(4), 371–418.

Frege, Gottolab. 1981/1997. 'Thought.' In *The Frege Reader*. Ed. Michael Beaney. Malden, MA: Balckwell.

Fumerton, Richard. 2002. *Realism and the Correspondence Theory of Truth*. Lanham, MD: Rowman & Littlefield.

Godfrey-Smith, Peter. 2002. 'Dewey on Naturalism, Realism, and Science'. *Philosophy of Science,* 69, S25–35.

Goodin, Robert E. 1992. *Green Political Theory.* Cambridge: Polity Press.

Goodman, Nelson. 1974/1955. *Fact, Fiction, and Forecast.* Cambridge, MA: Harvard University Press.

—1978. *Ways of Worldmaking.* Indianapolis: Hackett.

Green, Judith. 1999. *Deep Democracy.* Lanham: Rowman & Littlefield.

Gutmann, Amy and Thompson, Dennis. 2004. *Why Deliberative Democracy?* Princeton, NJ: Princeton University Press.

Haack, Susan. 1993. *Evidence and Inquiry.* Oxford: Blackwell.

—1998. 'Science as Social? – Yes and No'. *Manifesto of a Passionate Moderate.* Chicago: Chicago University Press.

Hardin, Russell. 2003. 'Street Level Epistemology and Democratic Participation'. In *Debating Deliberative Democracy.* James Fishkin and Peter Laslett, eds. Oxford: Blackwell.

Hickman, Larry. 1996. 'Nature as Culture: John Dewey's Pragmatic Naturalism'. In *Environmental Pragmatism.* Andrew Light and Eric Katz, eds. New York: Routledge.

Holden, Meg. 2001. 'Phenomenology versus Pragmatism: Seeking a Restoration Environmental Ethic'. *Environmental Ethics,* 22(1), 37–56.

Hookway, Christopher. 2002. *Truth, Rationality, and Pragmatism: Themes from Peirce.* Oxford: Oxford University Press.

Howell, Robert. 2005. 'A Puzzle for Pragmatism'. *American Philosophical Quarterly,* 42(2), 131–6.

James, William. 1977. *The Writings of William James.* John J. McDermott, ed. Chicago: University of Chicago Press.

—1996. *A Pluralistic Universe.* Lincoln: University of Nebraska Press.

Johnston, M. 1993. 'Verificationism as Philosophical Narcissism'. *Philosophical Perspectives,* 7, 307–30.

Kant, Immanuel. 1963. 'Our Duties to Animals'. In *Lectures on Ethics.* Louis Infield, trans. New York: Harper & Row.

Kirk, G. S. and Raven, J. F. 1962. *The Pre-Socratic Philosophers.* Cambridge: Cambridge University Press.

Kirkham, Richard. 1995. *Theories of Truth.* Cambridge, MA: MIT Press.

Kitcher, Philip. 2001. *Science, Truth, and Democracy.* Oxford: Oxford University Press.

Leopold, Aldo. 1977/1949. *A Sand County Almanac.* Oxford: Oxford University Press.

Light, Andrew. 1996. 'Compatibilism in Political Ecology'. In *Environmental Pragmatism.* Andrew Light and Eric Katz, eds. New York: Routledge. 161–84.

Lippmann, Walter. 1922. *Public Opinion.* New York: Free Press.

Lovejoy, A. O. 1908. 'The Thirteen Pragmatisms'. *The Thirteen Pragmatisms.* Baltimore: Johns Hopkins University Press.

Lynch, Michael. 2005. *True to Life: Why Truth Matters.* Cambridge, MA: MIT Press.

Mackie, Gerry. 2003. *Democracy Defended.* Cambridge: Cambridge University Press.

REFERENCES

Macpherson, C. B. 1973. 'Revisionist Liberalism'. *Democratic Theory: Essays in Retrieval*. New York: Oxford University Press.
Mansbridge, Jane. 1983. *Beyond Adversary Democracy*. Chicago: University of Chicago Press.
McCarthy, Thomas. 1989. 'Contra Relativism: A Thought Experiment'. In *Relativism: Interpretation and Confrontation*. Michael Krausz, ed. Notre Dame: University of Notre Dame Press. 256–70.
McDowell, John. 1994. *Mind and World*. Cambridge, MA: Harvard University Press.
Mill, John Stuart. 1991/1861. *Considerations on Representative Government*. Amherst, NY: Prometheus Books.
Mintz, Joel. 2004. 'Some Thoughts on the Merits of Pragmatism as a Guide to Environmental Protection'. *Boston College Environmental Affairs Law Review*, 31(1), 1–26.
Misak, Cheryl. 2000. *Truth, Politics, Morality*. New York: Routledge.
—2004a. *Truth and the End of Inquiry*. New York: Oxford University Press.
—2004b. 'Making Disagreement Matter'. *Journal of Speculative Philosophy*, 18(1), 9–22.
—2007. 'Pragmatism and Deflationism'. *New Pragmatists*. Oxford: Oxford University Press. 68–90.
Moore, G. E. 1903. *Principia Ethica*. Cambridge: Cambridge University Press.
Munnichs, Geert. 2002. 'Rational Politics?' In *Discourse and Democracy*. Rene Von Schomberg and Kenneth Baynes, eds. Albany, NY: SUNY Press.
Naess, Arne. 1973. 'The Shallow and the Deep, Long Range Ecology Movements: A Summary'. *Inquiry*, 16, 95–100.
—1995. 'Politics and the Ecological Crisis'. In *Deep Ecology for the 21st Century*. G. Sessions, ed. Boston: Shambahala.
Nagel, Thomas. 1980. 'Armstrong on the Mind'. In *Readings in Philosophy of Psychology*. Ned Block, ed. Cambridge, MA: Harvard University Press.
—2001. 'Pluralism and Coherence'. In *The Legacy of Isaiah Berlin*. Ronald Dworkin, Mark Lila, and Robert Silvers, eds. New York: New York Review of Books Press.
Nielson, Kai. 2007. 'Metaphilosophy, Pragmatism and a Kind of Critical Theory: Kai Nielen and Richard Rorty'. *Philosophical Papers*, 36(1), 119–50.
Nino, Carlos. 1996. *The Constitution of Deliberative Democracy*. New Haven, CT: Yale University Press.
Norton, Bryan. 1996. 'Integration or Reduction: Two Approaches to Environmental Values'. In *Environmental Pragmatism*. Andrew Light and Eric Katz, eds. New York: Routledge. 105–38.
Nozick, Robert. 1974. *Anarchy, State, and Utopia*. New York: Basic Books.
Parker, Kelly. 1996. 'Pragmatism and Environmental Thought'. In *Environmental Pragmatism*. Andrew Light and Eric Katz, eds. New York: Routledge. 21–37.
—2004. 'A Reply to C. A. Bowers'. *Environmental Ethics*, 26(3), 333–4.

Perry, Ralph Barton. 1948. *The Thought and Character of William James*. Cambridge, MA: Harvard University Press.

Phillips, Jamie. 2007. 'What Can a Drunk Really Know? Solving a Puzzle for Pragmatism'. *Southwest Philosophy Review*, 23(1), 181–9.

Popper, Karl. 1962. *Conjectures and Refutations: The Growth of Scientific Knowledge*. New York: Basic Books.

—1971. *The Open Society and Its Enemies*. Princeton, NJ: Princeton University Press.

Posner, Richard. 2002. 'Dewey and Democracy: A Critique'. *Transactional Viewpoints*, 1(3), 1–4.

—2003. *Law, Pragmatism, and Democracy*. Cambridge, MA: Harvard University Press.

—2004. 'Smooth Sailing'. *Legal Affairs* (January/February), 41–2.

Putnam, Hilary. 1975/1960. 'Minds and Machines'. *Mind, Language, and Reality*. Cambridge: Cambridge University Press.

—1996/1974. 'Philosophy and Our Mental Life'. In *Modern Philosophy of Mind*. William Lyons, ed. London: Everyman's Press.

—1997. 'James's Theory of Truth'. In *The Cambridge Companion to William James*. Ruth Anna Putnam, ed. Cambridge: Cambridge University Press.

Quine, Willard van Orman. 1953. 'Two Dogmas of Empiricism'. *From a Logical Point of View*. Cambridge, MA: Harvard University Press.

—1960. *Word and Object*. Cambridge, MA: MIT Press.

—1969. 'Epistemology Naturalized'. In *Ontological Relativity*. New York: Columbia University Press.

—1970. *Philosophy of Logic*. Englewood Cliffs, NJ: Prentice Hall.

—1981. *Theories and Things*. Cambridge, MA: Harvard University Press.

Ramsey, Frank. 1964/1927. 'Facts and Propositions'. In *Truth*. George Pitcher, ed. Englewood Cliffs, NJ: Prentice Hall.

Rawls, John. 1996. *Political Liberalism*. New York: Columbia University Press.

—1999a. *A Theory of Justice* (rev. edn). Cambridge, MA: Harvard University Press.

—1999b. 'The Idea of Public Reason Revisited'. In *John Rawls: Collected Papers*. Samuel Freeman, ed. Cambridge, MA: Harvard University Press.

Rescher, Nicholas. 1985. *The Strife of Systems: An Essay on the Grounds and Implications of Philosophical Diversity*. Pittsburgh, PA: Pittsburgh University Press.

—2001. *Cognitive Pragmatism: The Theory of Knowledge in Pragmatic Perspective*. Pittsburgh, PA: Pittsburgh University Press.

—2003. *Epistemology: An Introduction to the Philosophy of Knowledge*. Albany, NY: SUNY Press.

Rorty, Richard. 1967. 'Metaphilosophical Introduction'. In *The Linguistic Turn*. Richard Rorty, ed. Chicago: University of Chicago Press.

—1970. 'Incorrigibility as the Mark of the Mental'. *The Journal of Philosophy*, 67(12), 399–424.

—1979. *Philosophy and the Mirror of Nature*. Princeton, NJ: Princeton University Press.

—1982. *Consequences of Pragmatism.* Minneapolis: University of Minnesota Press.

—1983. 'Pragmatism without Method'. *Objectivity, Relativism, and Truth.* Cambridge: Cambridge University Press.

—1987. 'Science as Solidarity'. *Objectivity, Relativism, and Truth.* Cambridge: Cambridge University Press.

—1988. 'The Priority of Democracy to Philosophy'. *Objectivity, Relativism, and Truth.* Cambridge: Cambridge University Press.

—1989. *Contingency, Irony, Solidarity.* Cambridge: Cambridge University Press.

—1991. 'Solidarity or Objectivity?' *Objectivity, Relativism, and Truth: Philosophical Papers Volume 1.* Cambridge: Cambridge University Press.

—1996. 'Idealizations, Foundations, and Social Practices'. In *Democracy and Difference.* Seyla Benhabib, ed. Princeton, NJ: Princeton University Press.

—1998a. 'Pragmatism and Romantic Polytheism'. In *the Resurgence of Pragmatism.* Morris Dickstein, ed. Durham, NC: Duke University Press.

—1999. *Philosophy and Social Hope.* New York: Penguin.

Rosenthal, Sandra. 1996. 'Classical American Pragmatism: The Other Naturalism'. *Metaphilosophy,* 27, 317–40.

Rosenthal, Sandra and Buchholz, Rogene. 1996. 'How Pragmatism Is an Environmental Ethic'. In *Environmental Pragmatism.* Andrew Light and Eric Katz, eds. New York: Routledge. 161–208.

Russell, Bertrand. 1966/1908. 'William James's Conception of Truth'. *Philosophical Essays.* New York: Touchstone.

—1966/1909. 'Pragmatism'. *Philosophical Essays.* New York: Touchstone.

—1996/1946. *A History of Western Philosophy.* New York: Routledge.

Schmitt, Frederick. 1995. *Truth: A Primer.* Boulder, CO: Westview.

Schumpeter, Joseph. 1962. *Capitalism, Socialism, and Democracy.* New York: Harper Books.

Searle, John. 2004. *Mind: A Brief Introduction.* Oxford: Oxford University Press.

Sellars, Wilfrid. 1956/1997. 'Empiricism and Philosophy of Mind'. In *Minnesota Studies in the Philosophy of Science* (vol. 1). Herbert Feigl and Michael Scriven, eds. Minneapolis: University of Minnesota Press. Republished as *Empiricism and the Philosophy of Mind.* Cambridge, MA: Harvard University Press.

—1962. 'Truth and Correspondence'. *The Journal of Philosophy,* 59, 29–56.

—2007/1962. 'Philosophy and the Scientific Image of Man'. In *In the Space of Reasons.* Kevin Scharp and Robert Brandom, eds. Cambridge, MA: Harvard University Press.

—2007/1969. 'Language as Thought and Communication'. In *In the Space of Reasons.* Kevin Scharp and Robert Brandom, eds. Cambridge, MA: Harvard University Press.

—2007/1974. 'Meaning as Functional Classification'. In *In the Space of Reasons.* Kevin Scharp and Robert Brandom, eds. Cambridge, MA: Harvard University Press.

Shapiro, Ian. 2003. *The State of Democratic Theory*. Princeton, NJ: Princeton University Press.

Smith, John. 1999. 'Introduction'. In *Classical American Philosophy: Its Contemporary Vitality*. Sandra Rosenthal, Carl Hausman, and Douglas Anderson, eds. Urbana: University of Illinois Press.

Stich, Stephen. 1993. *The Fragmentation of Reason*. Cambridge, MA: MIT Press.

Stout, Jeffrey. 2007. 'Our Interest in Getting Things Right'. In *New Pragmatists*. Cheryl Misak, ed. Oxford: Oxford University Press. 7–31.

Strawson, P. F. 1959. *Individuals*. New York: Anchor Books.

Stuhr, John. 1998. 'Dewey's Social and Political Philosophy'. In *Reading Dewey*. Larry Hickman, ed. Indianapolis: Indiana University Press.

Talisse, Robert B. 2001. 'A Pragmatist Critique of Richard Rorty's Hopeless Politics'. *Southern Journal of Philosophy*, 39(4), 611–26.

—2003. 'Can Democracy Be a Way of Life? Deweyan Democracy and the Problem of Pluralism'. *Transactions of the C. S. Peirce Society*, 39(1), 1–21.

—2005. 'Deliberative Democracy Defended'. *Res Publica*, 11(2), 185–99.

—2007. *A Pragmatist Philosophy of Democracy*. New York: Routledge.

Talisse, Robert B. and Aikin, Scott F. 2005a. 'Why Pragmatists cannot be Pluralists'. *Transactions of the C. S. Peirce Society*, XLI.1, 101–18.

—2005. 'Still Searching for a Pragmatist Pluralism'. *Transactions of the C. S. Peirce Society*, 41(1), 145–60.

Thayer, H. S. 1952. *The Logic of Pragmatism*. New York: Humanities Press.

—1981. *Meaning and Action*. Indianapolis: Hackett.

—1993. 'Objects of Knowledge'. In *Philosophy and the Reconstruction of Culture*. John Stuhr, ed. Albany, NY: SUNY Press.

Tiles, James. 1988. *Dewey*. New York: Routledge.

West, Cornel. 1986. 'Dispensing with Metaphysics in Religious Thought'. *Religion and Intellectual Life*, 3(3), 53–6.

—1989. *The American Evasion of Philosophy*. Madison: University of Wisconsin Press.

Whitehead, Alfred North. 1929. *Process and Reality*. New York: Macmillan.

Wiggins, David. 2002. 'An Indefinablist cum Normative View of Truth and the Marks of Truth'. In *What is Truth?* R. Schantz, ed. New York: W. de Gruyter.

INDEX

absolute idealism 3
actual occasions 103
Aeneid 60
Aikin, Scott F. 45, 176
Alston, William 176
analytic philosophy 3, 5
analytic/synthetic dichotomy
   123–4, 128
anthropocentricism 165, 170
anti-cognitivism 31–2, 38
anti-epistemology 35–6
anti-foundationalism 39, 44, 47,
   131
   political anti-foundationalism
   (Rorty) 141
Aristotle 7

belief 28–51
Bentham, Jeremy 7
Bernstein, Richard 25
biocentrism 165
Boghossian, Paul 176
Bohman, James 177
Boisvert, Raymond 177
Bowers, C. A. 168–9
Bradley, F. H. 102
Brandom, Robert 40, 43, 46–7
   rationalist pragmatism 43
Briggle, Adam 174
Bucholz, Rogene 167–8
Burke, Thomas 176
Bush, George W. 124, 151

Capps, John 176
Carnap, Rudolf 103–5
   internal and external
   questions 104, 106
Cartesian rationalism 3
Chalmers, David 176
Chomsky, Noam 154
Christ, Jesus 117
Christianity 117
Christiano, Thomas 178
Clanton, Caleb 93
Clinton, Bill 28, 81
closure principle 52
cognitive significance 55, 67
coherence 59, 60
Colapietro, Vincent 177
common faith (Dewey) 90, 94
community 137
comprehensive doctrines 137
concrescence 103
correspondence theory of
   truth 55, 77

Dahl, Robert 146
Davidson, Donald 40, 106
De Waal, Cornelis 64
deep ecology 170–2, 174
deflationism 78, 80–2
demand 111
democracy
   as way of life 133
   democratic foundationalism 141

MacPherson, C. B. 178
magic 8 ball 38
Mansbridge, Jane 178
Marx, Karl 7
materialism/spiritualism 11
McCarthy, Thomas 176
McDowell, John 40
meliorism 107, 110, 112, 114, 130
 James on 110
metalanguage 80
metaphysical neutrality 81
mild epistemarchy 156
Mill, John Stuart 140, 156, 161–2
minimal mutilation principle 132
Mintz, Joel 172
Misak, Cheryl 20, 62, 64, 82–3,
 133, 154–64
 on democracy 160
 on truth 157
monism 10, 102, 114, 173
Moore, G. E. 89
moral inquiry 107, 119, 128
moral intuitions 130
moral methodism 118–19
moral ontology 165
moral pluralism 112
morally problematic situation 121
Munnichs, Geert 178

Naers, Arne 170
Nagel, Thomas 117, 176
naturalism 85, 88, 107–8
naturalistic fallacy 89
nexus 103
Nielson, Kai 33, 35
Nietzsche, Friedrich 145
nihilism 100
 bundle theory 100
NIMBY phenomenon 146
Nino, Carlos 178
non-anthropocentricism 165, 170
non-reductive metaphysics 87
normative significance 56, 67

normativity 80
Norton, Bryan 172–4
Nozick, Robert 142–4
Nussbaum, Martha 140

objectivity 35
objects 99, 102
obligation 111

Parker, Kelly 167, 169–70
Parmenides 75
'passes for' fallacy 38
pattern of inquiry 120
Peirce, Charles Sanders 5–21,
 23–7, 30, 40, 61–6, 72,
 82–3, 86, 95, 107, 120, 154,
 157–60
 first rule of reason 30
 on foundationalism 27–9
 pragmatic maxim 9–11, 13, 20,
 61, 107
 on truth 21, 41, 62
 transubstantiation 10, 13, 87
perfectionism 134–5, 140
Pericles 63–4
Perry, Ralph Barton 25
perspective 50
phenomenology 3
Phillips, Jamie 176
philosopher kings 155, 161
Plato 155–6, 161–2
 epistemarchy 155, 157, 161
 philosopher kings 155, 161
plausibilism 44, 47
pluralism 100, 112, 114, 116
 moral 112
 political 135
 Rawls on 136–8
 reasonable pluralism 137–8
policy 49
political anti-foundationalism 141
political discourse 151
political pluralism 135